THE
LETTERBOXER'S
COMPANION

THE

LETTERBOXER'S

◇◇

COMPANION

Exploring the Mysteries Hidden in the Great Outdoors

SECOND EDITION

RANDY HALL

GUILFORD, CONNECTICUT
HELENA, MONTANA

AN IMPRINT OF GLOBE PEQUOT PRESS

To buy books in quantity for corporate use
or incentives, call **(800) 962–0973**
or e-mail **premiums@GlobePequot.com.**

FALCONGUIDES®

FalconGuides is an imprint of Globe Pequot Press.
Falcon, FalconGuides, and Outfit Your Mind are registered trademarks of Morris Book Publishing, LLC.

Illustrations: Diane Blasius; page 92, Lori Enik
All interior photos by Randy Hall
Stamp images: Pages x, 36, 41, 79 by legerdemaine; pp. 1, 52, 83 by Sarah Strickland; p. 2 by Samuel Purre; p. 6 by The Northerner; pp. 7, 76 by Alafair; p. 13 by Jay Drew; p. 55 by Deb McClurken, aka SpringChick; p. 55 by Kris Buquet, aka NewBel; p. 56 by author for illustrative purposes; p. 81 by Scarab of the Doubtful Guests.

Text design: Sheryl P. Kober
Project editor: Julie Marsh
Layout artist: Melissa Evarts

The Library of Congress has catalogued the previous edition as follows:
   Hall, Randy.
     The letterboxer's companion / Randy Hall.
       p. cm.
   Includes index
   ISBN 0-7627-2794-2
   1. Letterboxing (Game) I. Title.

   GV1202.L48H35 2004
   796.1'4—dc22

                                                                          2003060140

ISBN 978-0-7627-4679-8

Printed in the United States of America

10 9 8 7 6 5 4 3 2 1

For Lisa and Stevie

ACKNOWLEDGMENTS

Special thanks to those letterboxers—some listed here by their trail names—who graciously supplied their stamp art for this book: Alafair (*Mystery Gathering*, signature stamp); Kris Buquet, aka NewBe1 (*Paw Print Series*); Jay Drew (*Latimer Brook*); legerdemaine (*Flutterby, Gorham Mountain, Smithsonian*, and *Somes Pond*); The Northerner (signature stamp); Samuel Purre (*Letterbox at Cranmere Pool*); Sarah Strickland (*Devon Hitchhiker, Robin's Nest,* and *World Domination Hitchhiker*); Scarab of the Doubtful Guests (*The Inventor*); Deb McClurken, aka SpringChick (*Bridges of Lancaster*).

I would also like to thank the members of the LbNA talk list for their constant flow of ideas, and the mid-Atlantic area letterboxers for their imaginative letterboxes that provided inspiration while working on this book.

CONTENTS

Stamping up after the find.

INTRODUCTION TO LETTERBOXING

Nothing compares to the thrill of the hunt. You're hiking through a forest of ancient hemlocks on a forgotten road, following a trail of cunning riddles to something cryptically referred to as the "wizard of the wood." You check your compass, then spy a gnarled oak just upstream that looks eerily like an old man. At its feet you find the cubbyhole that you know will be there, and pull out a small box containing some of the most exquisite stamp art you've ever seen.

Letterboxing is an intriguing mix of hiking, puzzle solving, treasure hunting, and rubber stamp artistry, topped off with the thrill of discovery. The pastime can take you to stunning and special outdoor places you never knew existed, lead you through a maze of local history and lore, and challenge you with mind-boggling riddles and puzzles; or it can simply guide you on a fun, relaxing half-hour walk with the kids or the dog, or on a straightforward day hike through rugged wilderness.

There is something for everyone in this quaint old-world pastime. Artists and writers enjoy the opportunity to express themselves in their stamps and clues, while hikers and outdoor adventurers have found it an excellent way to share their special places with others. Letterboxing has been used for education, team building, and as a way to explore a community's heritage.

Gorham Mountain

Letterbox stamps can be quite artistic and often depict natural themes.

The idea is pretty simple. Letterbox clues lead you to the secret location of a box that contains a stamp and logbook. You carry with you your signature stamp and personal logbook. When you figure out the clues and find the box, you stamp the box's logbook with your signature stamp, and stamp your personal logbook with the box's stamp.

In addition to the thrill of the hike and the solving of the clues, it's fun to read the box's logbook and see who has been there before. You might also enjoy getting together with other letterboxers and comparing personal logbooks to see who has been where and to marvel over some of the stamp images people have discovered.

After the hunt you can log your finds and attempts on the Internet as part of a large and growing online letterboxing community, and track who is searching for your boxes. Or, if you prefer the more traditional secrecy aspects of the game, you can ignore the online logging entirely.

In this book I'll teach you the basics of letterboxing, without giving away too many secrets. I'll answer a lot of questions that have come up over the past few years, and show you some possibilities. From there, it is up to you where your creativity and sense of adventure take you.

- *You'll learn the history of letterboxing,* from its Dartmoor origins to its history in America.

- *You'll learn the basics of finding letterboxes,* including what you'll need, where to find clues, how to use a compass, and other navigation techniques.

- *You'll learn the basics of rubber stamp carving,* including what tools and media to use, how to transfer images, and how to mount stamps.

- *You'll learn the basics of constructing and hiding a letterbox,* including suitable materials to use and those to avoid, how to find a good place, and why some places are better than others.

- *You'll learn the basics of clue writing,* including some various styles of clues, and tips on the dos and don'ts of clue writing.

- *You'll learn the basics of letterboxing etiquette,* both on the trail and on the Internet.

- *You'll learn about some advanced techniques,* including hitchhikers, mysteries, cuckoos, and other oddities.

- *You'll learn about the large and growing online community of letterboxers,* and the important letterboxing resources on the web and how to use them to enhance your experience.

Once you've experienced the adventure of letterboxing, you'll discover that this fascinating pastime is open to your innovations.

History of Letterboxing

Legend has it that letterboxing was born in 1854 when a gentleman, while walking the moors of Dartmoor, Devon, England, placed his calling card in a jar by the remote Cranmere Pool. He is said to have left a note directing anyone who found his card to leave theirs as well. Word spread of this secret on the moors, and soon other "letterboxes" began showing up in Dartmoor. Over time, the cards were replaced by stamps, and clues were written up and passed around by word of mouth.

There has always been an air of mystique and secrecy surrounding the genteel pastime of Dartmoor letterboxing. In fact, it had been said that you first had to find one hundred boxes on the moor before you could even get ahold of the catalog of clues (this is not actually true). For this reason, the pastime didn't spread to the United States for many years,

The **Devon Hitchhiker** celebrates the birthplace of letterboxing in Dartmoor, Devon, England.

with the exception of a few boxes placed by Dartmoor letterboxers, the clues to which were distributed by word of mouth.

The first known organized letterboxing activity in the United States was pioneered by David Sobel of Antioch New England Graduate School in Keene, New Hampshire. His Valley Quest program, with origins dating to 1989, was started as a way to increase awareness of the heritage and natural splendor found in the Upper Valley region of New Hampshire and Vermont. This program is still going strong and has since spread to other communities.

The "modern" era of North American letterboxing was ushered in with the publication of an article on the pastime in *Smithsonian* magazine in April 1998. By the end of April, the first letterbox was placed on Max Patch Mountain in North Carolina, and a few days later *Prayer Rock,* the first box with a hand-carved stamp, was placed along the New Haven River in Bristol, Vermont. (This has been a source of controversy among a handful of letterboxers, who suggest Prayer Rock was created first but the Max Patch clues were merely written and published first. Like much of the rest of the hobby, this will remain shrouded in mystery.) A website and talk list were

This stamp depicts the location of the first letterbox ever—at Cranmere Pool.

set up on the Internet, and those who read the *Smithsonian* article found each other through these resources. They started a small community to post clues on the web and share stories of their adventures, and a sprinkling of boxes began appearing around the country and on the website.

Independently, in June 1998 the staff of an outdoor equipment store in Waterford, Connecticut, began placing boxes and posting clues at the store, and encouraged others to do the same. Letterboxing was soon a flourishing outdoor activity in southern New England. Shortly thereafter, the two groups discovered each other, and the Letterboxing North America (LbNA) community was born. Boxes were soon being hidden in all fifty states, Canada, and around the world, with clues published on the LbNA website (www.letterboxing.org). Run as a nonprofit association for the community by a group of volunteers, this website continues to be a main source of clues for North American letterboxes today.

As the pastime grew, so have the online resources and community. Atlas Quest (www.atlasquest.com, commonly known as "AQ"), for instance, has since grown to be the largest letterboxing-related website in terms of clues listed, by offering a host of modern features including enhanced logging, useful search and planning functions, and a mobile device–friendly interface.

The methods of American letterboxing, as well as geography, defined the way the activity evolved in contrast to Dartmoor letterboxing. Because clues are publicly posted on websites, they are readily available to anyone and the Internet remains a big part of the pastime. Information on Dartmoor techniques and conventions was sparse in the early days, so American letterboxing, which will be the focus of this book, evolved mostly on its own, while reinventing and varying some of the Dartmoor traditions with guidance from a few moorland wizards. The spread-out, wooded nature of the American outdoors led to a different style of clue than what had evolved on the open moors, where precision map and compass work is often necessary. The clue styles and techniques are often different between the two methods, but the mystique and charm of this old English pastime remain strong in American letterboxing.

Gearing Up to Find Letterboxes

A letterboxer can search for boxes or create them for others to find, but most enjoy doing both. Before placing boxes, however, it is a good idea to get your feet wet by finding a few. In this chapter I'll explain what you need to get started finding boxes; in the next chapter I'll go over some basic techniques.

WHAT YOU'LL NEED

- ❏ Signature stamp
- ❏ Personal logbook
- ❏ Ink pad
- ❏ Clues
- ❏ Compass
- ❏ Pen

You don't need a heavy investment in equipment to get started in this pastime.

These items are in addition to the usual hiking gear you will need.

Try not to skimp on your signature stamp. Aim for something distinctive or exquisite.

YOUR SIGNATURE STAMP

Your signature stamp is what you use to "stamp in" in the logbooks of letterboxes you find. It is a rubber stamp that is your signature in the letterboxing world. Creating a distinctive stamp that is "you" is part of the art of letterboxing. This is sometimes called your *personal stamp*.

Types of Stamps

You basically have three choices in rubber stamps: hand carved, store bought, and custom made. Most letterboxers carve their signature stamps by hand (you'll learn how to do this in Chapter 5). Premade rubber stamps can be purchased from arts and crafts stores and discount department stores. You can have a rubber stamp custom made, based on artwork you supply, for about $20; do an Internet search or look in the Yellow Pages under "Rubber Stamps."

TIP If you are eager to get started before learning how to carve stamps yourself, consider a custom-made stamp before buying a premade one. This stamp will be your signature for years to come; don't buy a premade stamp unless you see something that is really special. Don't skimp on your signature stamp. Although few will admit it publicly, there is a stigma against premade stamps.

How Big?

Try to limit your signature stamp to no larger than 2 by 2 inches. As you'll learn, space in letterboxes is precious, and the logbooks are often small. Some letterboxers have even taken to carrying a separate, much

Keep your signature stamp small—it can still be beautifully carved.

smaller stamp for those really small logbooks that you find from time to time, but this is not necessary for the beginner.

YOUR PERSONAL LOGBOOK

Your personal logbook is what you'll use to collect the images of stamps from the letterboxes you find and to write notes about your adventures. It is also where you'll show off all your finds at

Sketchbooks with unlined pages make the best logbooks.

gatherings. Look for a distinctive book that's small and rugged, with unlined acid-free pages. I recommend a small, hardbound art sketchbook, which can be found at arts and crafts stores. You can often find good journals with unlined pages in card shops and bookstores. While you may be eager to get started and grab the nearest thing handy, such as a small spiral-bound, ruled notebook, this is a mistake, as not only will it be flimsy in the field, but you will regret not starting with a high-quality logbook when you look back on your collection years later.

THE INK PAD

Although some letterboxes contain ink pads, most do not, so you will need to bring your own. They come in many shapes and colors and can be found in arts and crafts stores and the larger discount department stores. There are two main types of ink: dye-based and pigment-based. Quick-drying dye-based inks produce crisp images but can run in wet conditions; pigment-based inks dry more slowly but are fade-resistant and often have more vibrant colors. Although I find the dye-based inks more suitable for letterboxing, some people prefer the pigment-based ones. Make sure the ink pad you buy is acid-free. Most of the best stamps are intended to be stamped in multiple colors, so I carry several ink pads for this purpose or to choose the color I like for the stamp that I find.

THE COMPASS

You don't need to spend a lot of money on a compass for letterboxing. Get a simple baseplate compass. A fancy sighting mirror compass or a super-fast orienteering compass isn't necessary (unless you'll be letterboxing in Dartmoor, where a sighting compass is recommended). A typical hiker's baseplate compass costs about $10 to $15 at outdoor equipment stores. See Chapter 3 for more information on compasses.

THE CLUES

Most clues to letterboxes in America can be found on the Internet, in particular on the Atlas Quest (www.atlasquest.com) and LbNA (www.letterboxing.org) websites. To begin a letterboxing adventure, just find some clues for your area, download and print, and be on your way! For example, on Atlas Quest, simply type in your zip code, town, or address in the "Location-Based Search" box in the upper right-hand corner of the main page, and a list of clues will be displayed. Other personal websites also contain clues, and some organizations, such as Valley Quest (www.vitalcommunities.org/valleyquest), publish clue booklets (see Chapter 8, "Internet Resources," for more on this).

Finding clues hidden either in the field or on the web is also part of the game. There's nothing like opening a letterbox and finding an unpublished clue to another box hidden there! Clues are often passed around by word of mouth or are deviously hidden in other ways that you'll discover once you've been exploring the letterboxing landscape for a while.

> **TIP** Once you've got your letterboxing gear together, get a small day pack and make a letterboxing kit. Put your logbook in a waterproof bag or carrying case, and do the same for your other gear. Make sure you store your signature stamp separately from your other gear in its own bag, as ink from the stamp tends to get all over everything.

Basics of Finding Letterboxes

One of the most enjoyable aspects of letterboxing is figuring out the clues, especially in the solitude of a beautiful hiking trail. There's nothing as satisfying as that "ah" feeling when you connect a feature of the landscape to a cryptic phrase on your "treasure map." I'm not going to give you a cookbook for figuring out letterboxing puzzles; that would spoil the fun. I will, however, give you a few pointers to remember when hitting the trail in search of the next addition to your logbook.

CHOOSE THE RIGHT CLUES

Clues come in all shapes and styles, from the simple to the cryptic, the poetic to the bizarre. Some are stories, puzzles, riddles, or pictures. Many clues, however, are simple, straightforward hiking directions, such as "Follow the red-blazed trail up the mountain, head 20 steps on bearing 160 degrees from the summit, and look under the large egg-shaped boulder." This style of clue

TIP Letterbox with a partner, your kids, or a group. Not only is it safer, it's more fun to share in the solving of the clues and the discovery of the clue's landmarks along the way.

TIP Read the entire clue before setting out. Not only will this help in estimating the time you'll be out on the trail, but you'll avoid some surprises the clue writer may have laid out for you at the end of the hike, such as obscure words or pieces of information you'll need to collect along the way. For example: "Find the stone-circle trail and follow it widdershins to the weir, then follow a bearing of 20 times the number of footbridges you have crossed so far." It's frustrating to hike back 5 miles to count bridges or to realize you should have done some research beforehand, as you have no idea what *widdershins* means. Carrying a mobile device can help, but keep in mind that there is often no signal on many of these hikes.

TIP The Atlas Quest clue system lists icons to indicate whether a hike is required, its approximate length, whether the clue is a mind-bending puzzle, and so forth. This system can be a good guide in selecting clues to tackle when getting started.

TIP There are no centralized standards, nor does a third party formally review clues for accuracy or compliance with any rules or customs. Online logging by others who have attempted the box can be valuable in these regards, but not all clues allow logging, and not all letterboxers choose to log comments.

TIP Remember the way back to your car as you are solving the clues. Most clues do not tell you how to get back to the starting point. Using a GPS and setting a waypoint at your car can help.

is a good choice to start out with. Just follow the directions; the person who placed the box is perhaps sharing a favorite hike or a spectacular view with you. Other clues will be more cryptic and may require research before setting out. Some will have to

THE LETTERBOXER'S COMPANION

be deciphered once you get to the area—for example, "Turn toward the circle arrow at the white rook, and follow Horace Greeley." You will be able to figure out what that means only when you get there, or you may have to do research before you set out. Many clues will require navigational techniques, such as using a compass with or without a map, triangulation, pacing, map reading, and so on. Learn these techniques before choosing the sorts of clues that require them. I will explain some of these later in this book.

The Latimer Brook stamp captures the essence of a beautiful hike.

ESTIMATE THE DIFFICULTY

It's easy to get caught up in the romance of treasure hunting, but letterboxing is, above all, a hiking pastime. It's important to determine the length and difficulty of the hike before setting out, and prepare yourself accordingly. Many clue writers will provide an estimated length of the hike, the difficulty rating, descriptions of the terrain, and other details; others will not.

These can be good guidelines, but keep in mind that everyone is at a different level of hiking fitness. You may be slowed down as you try to figure the clues, or you might make wrong turns along the way. So it's a good idea to get to know the area and come up with your own estimates of the hike before choosing a particular clue and setting out.

Take notes along the way. If the clue instructs you to take note of when a particular building was built, which might be required to calculate a pace count and bearing, write it down. You won't want to get 3 miles farther down the trail and find you don't remember the information when you need it.

USING A COMPASS

Many letterbox clues require proficiency with a compass. Using a compass is really quite simple once you get the hang of it, and most of these clues require nothing more than the simplest technique of following a bearing. I'll explain how to do that, then cover some advanced techniques.

Following a Compass Bearing

A clue might say, "From the square rock, follow a bearing of 314 degrees to the hidden pathway." (The terms *heading* and *azimuth* are sometimes used instead of *bearing*.) Turn the dial on the compass so the number 314 on the housing lines up with the

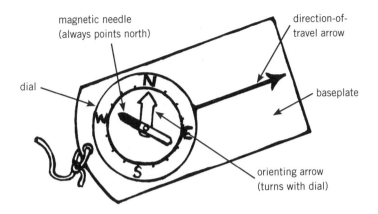

The important parts of a baseplate compass.

direction-of-travel arrow on the baseplate. This is called *dialing in the bearing.* Holding the compass flat and steady, turn your body until the red of the magnetic needle aligns with the red of the orienting arrow below it (some people use the mnemonic "put red in the shed" to remember this). The direction-of-travel arrow on the baseplate now indicates which way to go. That's all there is to it.

> **TIP** Be careful when using a compass near iron or magnetic objects, as these things will affect the needle and give you bad bearings. (There is, however, at least one letterbox clue that intentionally requires shooting bearings around large iron artifacts; be wary of devious clue writers playing with the basics of the pastime!)

FOLLOWING A BEARING

direction-of-
travel arrow

For better accuracy, head
for a distinct landmark in
the direction of travel.

You could just follow the direction-of-travel arrow while keeping the red of the needle aligned with the red of the orienting arrow until you find the "hidden pathway." However, a more accurate way to follow a bearing is to find a specific landmark in the exact direction indicated by the direction-of-travel arrow, such as a distinct tree or boulder, and head for that landmark. This is less error-prone and frees you to concentrate on pacing, triangulating, or looking for other landmarks mentioned in the clue. When you reach the landmark, verify that your needle is still aligned, and choose another landmark in the direction of the direction-of-travel arrow.

Bearings in letterboxing are only as accurate as the people who write them, some of whom may not be as proficient with a compass as you are. If you think you've done everything right but you still don't find what you're looking for, it may be that the clue is inaccurate or vague (whether intentionally or not), so be flexible and look around the area.

Magnetic Declination

Magnetic declination, a complication when using a compass, rarely needs to be accounted for in letterboxing, but you should know what it is and how to account for it in case you run into it.

Magnetic declination is basically a discrepancy caused by the fact that the magnetic north pole, which compasses use, and the geographic north pole are not in the same place. For example, when you follow a "north" bearing on a compass, you could be heading 10 degrees east of true north. The discrepancy varies from 0 to 20 degrees in the continental United States, depending on location. It also varies over time.

Almost all letterboxing clue writers simply read the bearing off a compass dial when writing clues, which means you only have to dial in the bearing they give you, ignoring declination.

TIP Sometimes declinations are given as negative or positive values. Positive values are degrees east, and negative values are degrees west. To avoid confusion, drop the minus sign, and use the above rule. (Alternatively, you can keep the minus sign, and use this equation: magnetic bearing = true bearing − magnetic declination.)

Some even say "all bearings magnetic" or something similar, which again is a signal to keep it simple. When in doubt, don't worry about declination.

Occasionally, however, you will run into a clue that reads, "All bearings are true" or "You must account for declination." In this case, you will need the general location and the time the box was placed, and you will have to research the declination for that area. (There are websites that will compute declination for you; see Chapter 8, "Internet Resources.")

Declination will be given as "degrees east" or "degrees west." If it is given as degrees west, add the declination to the given true bearing and dial that bearing into your compass. If given as degrees east, subtract the declination from the bearing given in the clue before dialing.

Triangulation and Back Bearings

The use of triangulation and back bearings is the opposite of following a bearing from a given spot to find a landmark: You are given landmarks and bearings that will help you find a certain location. These techniques are often used as an artistic way to give clues a quaint "treasure hunting" feel, or to write a more narrative style of clue, as opposed to simply giving directions. Typically, to take a back bearing, you start with the given bearing and add or subtract 180 (so that the result is less than 360), or you aim your direction-of-travel arrow at the given landmark on the given bearing and walk backward.

THE LETTERBOXER'S COMPANION

TRIANGULATION

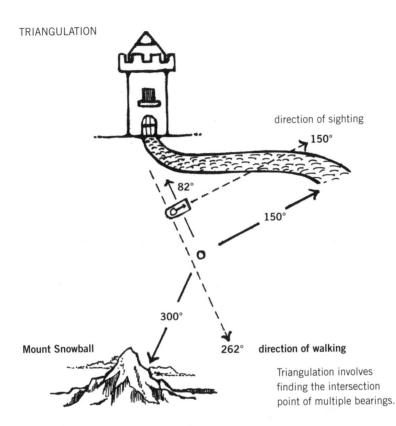

direction of sighting

150°

82°

150°

O

300°

Mount Snowball

262° direction of walking

Triangulation involves finding the intersection point of multiple bearings.

A simple example might be along these lines: "All she remembered from the old map fragment was that the brass ring could be found where Mount Snowball rose at 300 degrees, the wizard's tower sat at 82 degrees, and the old road dead-ended at azimuth 150."

Once you've recognized these landmarks, the idea is to take back bearings off one or more of them and triangulate to the spot from which each can be seen at the given bearings. For example, if you can start at the wizard's tower, follow a bearing of 262 (82 + 180) from there, and look for the other landmarks. To know when you are at the right place, stay on your given 262 bearing from the tower, dial in the bearing of one of the other landmarks (for example, 150 degrees), and turn your compass until the red of the needle aligns with the red of the orienting arrow. Keep walking your original line from the tower until the direction-of-travel arrow points to the landmark at 150 degrees, in this case, the old road endpoint. You should be at the right spot; look down to claim your treasure.

Typically, you only need two properly situated landmarks to triangulate to a point; it is basically the intersection of the two bearings. But you can verify the third landmark in the same way. In this case, dial in 300, turn the compass until the red of the needle aligns with the red of the orienting arrow, and the direction-of-travel arrow should point to Mount Snowball if you are at the right spot.

TIP To find the bearing of a given landmark from a particular spot, point the direction-of-travel arrow at the landmark, and turn the dial until the red of the needle aligns with the red of the orienting arrow. The number on the dial at the direction-of-travel arrow is the bearing of that landmark from that spot.

THE LETTERBOXER'S COMPANION

If you can't start at one of the landmarks, dial in the bearing of one of them (such as the tower), turn the compass until the red of the needle aligns with the red of the orienting arrow, and walk around until the direction-of-travel arrow points to that landmark, while keeping the needle aligned with the orienting arrow. The direction-of-travel arrow now represents the original line from the tower as in the preceding example. Proceed as in that example with the next landmark.

PACE COUNTING

Many clues measure distance in "paces" rather than in absolute measures such as feet. Perhaps this is to capture a feeling of hunting for lost pirate treasure (as pirates wrote their treasure maps using paces), or perhaps it is simply easier for clue writers to pace off a distance rather than measure it. Whatever the reason, pace counting is often a source of confusion for beginning letterboxers.

The problem is that no one seems to be sure if a pace is one step or two steps, and stride length varies significantly from person to person. (It was fine for pirates, because they wrote the maps for themselves, not for others to find their treasure.)

The official definition of a pace is two steps, but most American letterboxers count a pace as a single step. So if you are unsure, assume a pace in the clue means a single step. The real trick to pace counting, whether or not the clue is written using steps or paces, is to calibrate your pace to that of the clue writer.

Calibrating is pretty straightforward: Count how many of your paces (or steps) equal the clue writer's paces between easily identifiable landmarks, and use this ratio when you don't have obvious landmarks to work with.

For example, the clue may say, "Walk 50 paces from the Green Bird on a bearing of 322 to the Circle Circle, 30 paces west, then 40 paces on a bearing of 358 to a large tree." In this case—assuming you can figure out what the Green Bird and Circle Circle are referring to—if it takes you 75 paces to walk between them (whether you count a pace as one or two steps is up to you—just be consistent), you know it will take about 45 of your paces to walk the westerly second leg, and 60 to walk between that point and the tree (you are walking 3 paces for every 2 paces the hider walked in his clue, so multiply the hider's pace count by 3 and then divide by 2). Once you've calibrated your pace to a particular clue writer, remember that ratio for future clues by that planter. In this case, we know a ratio of 1.5 to 1 works for this letterboxer's clues.

Most good clue writers will give you some way to determine their pace, or the number will be so small (for example, 10 paces) that it will not be a problem in practice. Once in a while you

> **TIP** Calibrate your own pace to a fixed distance (for example, 100 feet). Then, when you encounter a clue that gives distances in feet, you will be able to estimate the distance by pacing it off.

will be stumped; try again, counting a pace as two steps, or try to find a different box. Sometimes online comment logging on that box will give it away or mention any problems with the pace counting, but you may consider this "cheating" to read such comments before setting out.

FINDING THE BOX

Once you've figured out the clues and know where the box is (for example, "the nook in the twin-trunked tree"), be careful of snakes, spiders, and other wildlife when reaching for it. Poke around the area with a stick to make sure nothing nasty lurks there.

Leave No Trace

If the box isn't where you expect it to be, don't dig around, root up mountains of rocks or old logs, or tear up stone walls looking for buried treasure. Most clues—if you can figure them out—will tell you precisely how to find the box. Leave your spade at home; you should never need to dig for a letterbox. If you don't find the box, reread the clues and look around; it's possible you've misinterpreted something.

It is important to leave the area exactly as you found it so others can enjoy its unspoiled state as well. If you can't find the box with a no-impact search, move on to another one; there are thousands to choose from.

However, if you are absolutely certain you have figured it out and are in the right spot—for example, you see a suspicious pile of rocks (SPOR) or a box-shaped indentation in the ground—contact the placer on the website where the clue was listed, identifying the feature you found, or log the box as "attempted" to give feedback that there may be a problem. Most placers, and the letterboxing community at large, like to be aware of when a box has gone missing, so a replacement can be made or the clues removed from the web. Keep in mind, however, that more often than not, boxes are mistakenly reported as missing due to mistakes in interpreting the clues, so double-check the clues first before reporting a box missing.

Stamping Up

The fun isn't over once you've found the box. Take the time to read through the logbook to see who was there before, and look for signature stamps you've never seen. A lot of the fun is the "virtual meeting" of other letterboxers through the logbook. Stamp in, and add a message of your own. Ink up the box's stamp and add it to your logbook.

Be discreet when stamping up. Don't give away the location of the box to others who may be passing by. Take the box to a

> **TIP** Wild animals pick up on food scents, so wash your hands well between eating and letterboxing. Food scents transferred to letterboxes attract animals, which sometimes drag a box out of its hiding place, causing it to be lost or damaged.

TIP Stamp something other than your logbook first (your clue sheet, for instance), so you will get an idea of what the stamp looks like and how it takes the ink. Moreover, many stamps are intended to take different color inks on the various parts of the images. Advanced letterboxers carry all number of colored inks so they can get the exact image that was intended. Experiment first before putting a messy or incorrectly colored image in your logbook.

secluded location where you can sit down and enjoy the contents. Put the box back *exactly* where you found it, and hide it as well as or better than it was originally hidden. Sometimes a box will become exposed over time; it's a service to the letterboxing community to re-hide it so that there is no chance of accidental discovery, but make sure you hide it as the original hider intended.

BOX REPAIR

Letterboxes will become damaged over time; the boxes crack, the logbooks become wet, and the internal bags some people use for waterproofing get torn. Carry some repair supplies with you, such as empty containers, spare bags, and perhaps even a spare logbook. Keep these items in your day pack. Make repairs when you encounter a damaged letterbox in the field, and (optionally) contact the person who placed the box. If you don't have the supplies with you, you should still contact the placer to indicate that a box needs maintenance. Others will be repairing your boxes for you if they find them damaged. (More on the supplies you will need is in the next chapter, "Basics of Creating Letterboxes," and contacting the placer is discussed a bit more in the "Etiquette" and "Internet Resources" chapters.)

OTHER CONSIDERATIONS

Finally, here are some other things you need to consider while planning or while on a letterboxing adventure.

Hiking Safety

As mentioned previously, letterboxing is primarily a hiking pastime, so be aware of hiking safety rules. Such considerations are beyond the scope of this book, but do heed the following precautions:

- Know the dates of game-hunting seasons in the area of the box. Dress appropriately (wear blaze orange), or better yet, choose another box.

- Be aware of dangerous wildlife in the area, such as bears or snakes, and know how to handle encounters with them.

- Learn how to recognize and avoid dangerous plants such as poison oak and poison ivy.

- Be aware of the local insects and insect-borne diseases (such as Lyme disease), and prepare accordingly.

- Check the weather forecast, and plan accordingly.

- Notify someone of where you'll be going and when you expect to be back. Use trail registries. Carry your cell phone.

Route Choice and Your Responsibilities

You, and not the person who placed the box, are responsible for your actions and route choice to the box. Don't assume that you have permission to go where a box has been placed or to take a particular route there, or that it is even safe to go there.

Don't trample sensitive vegetation or other unspoiled areas to get to a letterbox. Don't trespass. If you are not sure, ask. Observe all local rules, regulations, signs, laws, and customs. If it looks like the clues are leading you somewhere you're not supposed to be, use common sense—don't assume the clues are right. You may have misinterpreted the clues, you might be lost, the clues may have errors, or trail conditions and access rights may have changed since the box was placed.

Be alert for the hiding places nature provides.

Basics of Creating Letterboxes

After you've found a couple of boxes, you'll probably have a few ideas of your own for fun clues or for sharing a special place for others to discover. There are four elements to creating a letterbox:

- The Place

- The Stamp

- The Clues

- The Hardware

While each of these elements can be an art form in and of itself, the most stunning boxes are those for which the place, clues, and stamp work together to create something that is almost magical.

Often the best method is to think of the place, stamp art, and style of the clue together as a general concept. Then visit the place, find an actual hiding place, and work out the details or directions of the clues.

THE PLACE

Everything flows from the place. The best letterboxes lead you on a hunt through breathtaking wilderness, interesting historical, cultural, or educational sites, remote mountains or islands that are a challenge to get to, or simply to a very special or unknown place you'd like to share with others. Interesting geography or features in the terrain often lead to the most fascinating clues as well as provide inspiration for the stamp art. The place doesn't necessarily have to be a remote wilderness; city parks, small preserves, and even playgrounds can make good locations, especially for children.

After locating that special place, find the general area where you wish to place the box and get to know it better. Visualize how the clues will work overall; then find the exact location where you'd like to hide the box. For the hiding spot, find a cool location like a distinct tree, an interesting rock formation, or other unique terrain feature that will be easy for seekers to notice, be

TIP Try to find a place where there aren't many (or any) boxes. Due to the explosive growth of both letterboxing and geocaching over the past several years, some places have become cluttered with boxes and perhaps a geocache as well, leading to confusion among those seeking them. The main letterboxing websites allow you to do a location-based search, and while this won't find everything in the area, it is a good way to help find an untapped location that will allow your box to stand out.

an interesting place to hang out while stamping up, and make for good wordplay when writing the clue. Work backward from the hiding place, at least part of the way. You don't want to hike down the trail, finish writing your clues, and *then* look around for a hiding place in the small area your clues lead to. Good hiding places are sometimes difficult to find, and they often don't turn up when or where you want them to.

The Hiding Place

There are three primary considerations when choosing a hiding place:

- Choose a place where there is no chance of accidental discovery.

- Choose a place where there will be zero impact on the environment.

- Choose a place that is safe and legal.

The best hiding places are under rocks and ledges. The heavy rocks keep the box in place, and there is no visible change to the environment, which is not only a worthy goal in and of

TIP If your box is small enough, a good way to hide it is to lift a rock out of the ground, place the box in the cavity left by the rock, and replace the rock.

TIP Consider how your location will look in a different season. For example, what looks like a secluded, uncrowded area in the winter might be crawling with people in the summer, and what seems to be a well-hidden location in the summer could be wide open in the winter when all the vegetation is dead.

itself, but it helps keep the box safe from accidental discovery by passersby, vandals, and foraging animals. Rocks make solid, long-term, solid locations for planting boxes.

Hollow logs, stumps, and nooks in trees can make decent choices, but these tend to be less solid and more easily disturbed. Laying a box on the ground and covering it with leaves, twigs, and other debris is generally the poorest choice; boxes hidden in this way tend to be the first to go missing, if not from accidental discovery, then from foraging animals. Hiding an unanchored box near a river is just asking for it to be swept away at the next high water. Regardless of where your box is hidden, make sure it is anchored down.

Choose an area that is free from crowds. Well off-trail can be a good choice, provided a social trail to the box will not develop, and that such a placement would not violate local regulations.

Environmentally Friendly Hiding Places

Although the people who will be hunting for your box are responsible for their own actions, you should choose a place that is environmentally friendly. Common sense goes a long way here: Don't choose a place where the seeker would be tempted to trample sensitive flowers or otherwise disturb the area to get to your box. If you expect a lot of visitors, either because the clues will be straightforward or the box is in a populated location, choose a hiding place very near the trail so that a social trail doesn't develop. In this case it is especially important to find a solid, well-concealed location.

Choose an obvious feature to hide the box under. Don't leave a clue that says, "30 steps on bearing 20 from the trailhead, under a rock." Rocks make great hiding places, but if you can't find a distinctive rock, look for a hiding place that will allow you to say something like, "30 steps on bearing 20 to the large tree with the eye-shaped nook." There are lots of nondescript rocks in the forest, so if you don't make the hiding place obvious to someone who has figured out the clues, you could have people tearing up the forest floor looking under every rock. In addition to adding luck to the hunt and frustration for the seekers, this goes against the zero-impact ethics of letterboxing. Above all, don't dig a hole to bury your box, requiring others to dig for it.

Keep It Safe and Legal

Some things go without saying, but make sure the seeker can get to your box without going through poison ivy, scaling dangerous cliffs, trespassing, and so on. Likewise, make sure it is legal to place the box in the spot you have chosen. For example, it is against regulations to place letterboxes in national parks, national wildlife refuges, and other locations. Ask permission of the land manager or owner. Although some locations are supposedly off-limits to letterboxing, success has been reported in placing letterboxes in these areas when the person placing them has worked with the land managers.

As letterboxing and related hobbies such as geocaching have become increasingly popular, more and more parks and land managers are regulating their placement. Some parks require approval of the hiding place and clues by the local rangers, and others ban placement altogether, in some cases because of the careless behavior of previous letterboxers. Always check for these regulations, either on signs at the park, on the park's website, or with the rangers themselves. Violating local regulations may not only lead to a citation for yourself, but it gives the entire pastime a bad name.

Note that the Letterboxing North America (LbNA) terms of use require permission from the land manager for any box listed on the website. The terms of use on Atlas Quest are not as strict, but it is still necessary to verify that it is legal to place the letterbox where you have hidden it. Both websites have resources describing land manager policies.

Verify That There Are No Other Letterboxes or Geocaches in the Area

Geocaching is a pastime similar to letterboxing, where GPS devises are used to search for stashed containers (geocaches). GPS coordinates are listed on websites, the primary one being www.geocaching.com.

These pastimes have become so popular that it is possible that there is already a letterbox or geocache in the spot you have selected. It is important to attempt to verify that this isn't the case, as participants often confuse the two and find the wrong box or geocache. Geocachers might even take your hand-carved stamp, as part of that game involves taking things from the containers.

It is best to search your location on www.geocaching.com to make sure there is no geocache there, and search on AQ and LbNA to verify that there is not another letterbox already there. Some people get annoyed if you "poach" their location, and the location will be less unique anyway if people have just been there to find someone else's box or cache.

Respect Spiritual Places

It is rarely appropriate to place boxes in Native American burial grounds, earthworks, or other ceremonial or sacred sites; houses of worship; or cemeteries. Don't turn sacred spiritual places into recreational treasure hunts.

Indoor Hiding Places

Some of the most interesting and beguiling letterboxes have been placed indoors. Pubs, hollowed-out books in libraries and musty old used-book stores, and other intriguing locations have been used. Let your imagination run wild, but make sure you work it out with the building's owner first.

THE STAMP

Ideally, the stamp image you create or choose for your box will relate to the place or the clue in some way. For example, the image of the mountain your box is hidden on, or simply the name of that mountain, is an appropriate stamp image. That is part of the art of creating letterboxes; the stamp gives the box its personality and cachet. It's not essential for the stamp to relate—any image will do—but it is not a letterbox unless it includes a stamp of some sort for the finders of your box to stamp in their logbooks.

Many stamps relate to, or even name, the place where they are hidden.

As with the signature stamp, there are three choices for the box's stamp: hand carved, store bought, and custom made. There is no denying the fact that most letterboxers prefer to find hand-carved stamps. In fact, it has been said that it is preferable to find a poorly made hand-carved stamp rather than a store-bought one. For some people, it's about the place and the clues, and they will still look for your box if it doesn't contain a hand-carved stamp, but the hobby has evolved so that the most sought-after boxes are those with artistic, handcrafted stamps. This contrasts somewhat with Dartmoor letterboxing, in which custom-made stamps are more prevalent.

If you're not a stamp carver, team up with someone who is. You write the clues; your partner carves the stamp. Or turn lemons into lemonade; not confident creating artistic images, some people have taken to carving fragments of clues into stamps (this and other advanced techniques are discussed in Chapter 7).

Chapter 5 is dedicated entirely to making hand-carved stamps.

THE CLUES

Like the hand-carved stamp, letterbox clues can get fairly artistic, using rhymes, stories, riddles, puzzles, treasure maps, cryptic narratives, and so forth. Some clues are clever or tricky, and some are maddeningly difficult, but there is no taboo against simple directions to a park or trailhead followed by straightforward directions to the box. In fact, a large percentage of clues are written this way.

Look at other clues to see what styles you like; then work with your chosen place to lead people through the most beautiful and interesting areas it has to offer. Included in this section are some techniques that often make clues better and more fun for the letterboxers following them.

Confirming Landmarks

After a long hiking segment or a particularly difficult or confusing section of a riddle or puzzle clue, it is nice to include a confirming landmark to assure the letterbox seekers that they are on the right track. How you work it into your narrative is up to you, but it usually is a distinct, unique landmark that people will know when they see it—and know when they don't see it. Confirming landmarks are particularly useful at the starting point of mystery clues (see Chapter 7). They can also make the clue more interesting and fun, especially for kids.

For example: "Follow the trail, turn left at the second side trail, then bear right at the Y junction, watch out for the scary green monster, and continue. . . ." Seekers might not know what the "scary green monster" is until they pass it on the trail, but it will be a fun thing to look for, and it will serve to confirm that they didn't miss a turn along the way.

Confirming landmarks can be cryptic, visible only to those who have solved your puzzle. For example, one of my clues has

> **TIP** Landmarks can sometimes change quite suddenly. Dead trees fall or are removed by park rangers, stumps are removed, old logs rot away, and new trails are added. If you are looking for some longevity to your clues, consider landmarks that are less likely to disappear. Distinct living trees, boulders, and other rock features tend to last longer than old rotting trees, stumps, and logs.

THE LETTERBOXER'S COMPANION

TIP Consider avoiding use of the term *pace* when giving distances in clues. Use *step* instead; most letterboxers prefer this, and it avoids the ambiguity of what a *pace* is (as discussed in Chapter 3). Also, the use of steps is preferable to absolute measures such as feet, which many hikers will be unequipped to figure in the field.

a landmark called the "Joey Stone," which will confirm you've solved the crux of the puzzle. This landmark will only be apparent if the seeker is fairly confident he or she is in the right place, and will be impossible to locate otherwise.

Catching Features

Catching features, landmarks that tell seekers if they've gone too far, can be used when your directions are straightforward or not intended to be too difficult. These can be cryptic also, but typically they are along the lines of "If you've hit the stream, you've gone too far."

Pace Calibration Legs

If you are using paces to give your clues a treasure-hunt feel or as a convenient measure of distance, or even if you are following the recommendation to use steps instead, keep in mind that everyone's pace (or step) length, and even how they count them, is different. Because 50 paces (or steps) to you could be 75 to the person looking for your box, you may want to include what is called a pace calibration leg so the seeker can adjust his or her pace count to your pace count.

The basic idea is to provide your pace count between two landmarks so the seeker can compare his pace count to yours; for every two paces in the clue, someone else might need to take three steps. These can be worked into the narrative unobtrusively, and can make your clues more fun by having more landmarks to look for or puzzle out. The landmarks can serve double duty as confirming landmarks.

For example: "Follow the green path 200 paces to the Circle W, then 400 paces east into the woods to your reward." You don't need the 200 paces *and* the Circle W landmark, but including both will allow the seekers to calibrate so they know what 400 paces will be to them. (If it takes them 300 paces to walk to the Circle W, then they know they need three paces for every two in the clue, or 600 to walk from the Circle W to the box.)

Obvious Hiding Place

Describe the hiding place in such a way that it is obvious to someone who has figured out the clues. Consider making the last leg short, include a confirming landmark, and use a distinctive log or rock, so when other letterboxers figure out the clues, they are not greeted with many piles of rocks to search through. State explicitly how the box is hidden. This can still be cryptic, as long as it isn't vague.

Go for the "Ah" Experience

This is hard to describe, but you'll know it when you experience it. Nothing compares to the satisfaction of connecting cryptic directions to a landmark in the woods, or figuring something out and receiving confirmation that you're on the right track. This can be a lot of fun for letterboxers following your clues.

There is no easy way to describe how to do this, but giving seekers something to figure out, notice, or

Smithsonian

This letterbox pays homage to the Smithsonian article that ushered in the modern era of North American letterboxing.

connect, as opposed to straightforward directions or descriptions of landmarks and terrain features, is a good way to start. For example, rather than describe a landmark as "the large, round, white building," you might refer to it as "Mount Snowball." This is a very basic example, and keep in mind that doing this will make your clues more difficult. However, these kinds of clues can be as sophisticated and clever as your creativity allows, making the clue writing experience more fun for you. And, more important, you'll be providing seekers with the "ah" experience.

Educational Opportunities

A lot of the fun of letterboxing is what kids and adults alike can learn about the historical, cultural, and environmental treasures that can be discovered by following the clues. Clues can be educational in and of themselves, requiring you to identify particular types of trees along the trail or read a plaque about the history of a particular building and remember some fact about it later in the clue.

Writing style can make clues more educational. For example, compare "from the top of Mount Davis in Pennsylvania" and "from the highest point in Pennsylvania." Both styles accomplish the same thing, but the latter requires research and gives the opportunity to learn that Mount Davis is the high point in Pennsylvania.

As another example, consider "find the monument marking what some historians regard as the turning point of the

Revolutionary War, General Washington's departure point on Christmas night, 1776." The clues could be just as fun with straightforward directions to the monument and then on to the next landmark, but when written like this they offer an educational opportunity as well as a letterbox hunt. Taken a step further, rather than the above wording, you could weave this clue fragment into a story: "A soldier accompanying Washington on his departure this night was carrying something. What was it? Where did he lose it?" You can see how a story-style clue with an educational or historical theme can begin to develop. Go scout the place to see what works, and your story may flow.

Make Sure There Is a Safe, Legal Route

Conditions and access rights change, and route choice and responsibility rest with the seeker, but a safe, legal, trespass-free route to the box should be provided, and the intended interpretation of your clues should follow such a route.

Throw in a Compass Bearing

Many clues work just as well without compass use, but there is anecdotal evidence that boxes that require the seeker to own and know how to use a compass are less prone to vandalism. I personally don't feel this is too important, but it is something to consider. In general, boxes with harder clues will be less prone to going missing, and while compass bearings don't necessarily make clues harder for letterboxers, they do for prospective vandals.

In order to add bearings to your clues (for example, from landmark 1, head bearing X to landmark 2), stand with your back to the first landmark and face the second landmark, which need not actually be mentioned in your clue. Hold your compass flat and aim the direction- of-travel arrow at landmark 2. Then turn the dial until the red of the needle aligns with the red of the orienting arrow and read the number off the dial at the base of the direction-of-travel arrow. This is the bearing to mention in your clue. See Chapter 3 for more on compass use.

Other Considerations

The list below suggests some helpful information you might want to include with your clues. Seekers are always responsible for determining this information for themselves before setting out, but many (especially those with special interests or circumstances) will appreciate having it up front when deciding which boxes to search for.

- How many miles is the hike?

- How difficult is the terrain?

- How difficult are the clues?

TIP The Atlas Quest letterboxing website supports the flagging of clues with some of these facts, along with other information.

- Are dogs allowed on the trail or in the park?

- Is the box wheelchair accessible?

- Are the hike, area, and clues kid-friendly?

- Can the search be done on a mountain bike or skis?

- Is there a fee to enter the area?

- Is game hunting allowed in the area?

- Are there other hazards, such as poison ivy or bears, to consider?

Publication and Distribution of Your Clues

Most letterboxing clues in North America are distributed on the Internet; your clues will reach the most people if they are posted there. The main sites for publishing clues are Atlas Quest (www .atlasquest.com) and LbNA (www.letterboxing.org). You will need to set up a free account before publishing clues on either site. As of now, Atlas Quest has more users, more clues, and more features. Creating clues on either website is straightforward. (See more on these websites in Chapter 8.)

Alternatively, if you are handy creating and hosting web pages, you can publish your clues in your own web space. This gives you greater artistic control of the clues. Both major websites allow you to publish links to your clues, or you can keep your self-published clues "underground" by not linking to these sites. While there are some personal underground clue sites, the vast majority of clues (or links to them) are published on one of the major sites, and this is the best option for letterboxers who are just starting out.

Clues can also be distributed by word of mouth or by other interesting means, such as in other boxes as cuckoos or bonuses (see Chapter 7), hidden in cryptic posts on the various Internet letterboxing forums, or snuck into books on letterboxing.

THE HARDWARE

The actual box and its contents are usually the easiest part; most letterboxers find materials that work for them and keep using them. However, even the box can be part of the art. Letterboxes in

Basic letterboxes are fairly simple and inexpensive to construct.

hollowed-out books, small candy tins, and handcrafted wooden boxes have been spotted.

There are three primary considerations for constructing a letterbox:

- Make it waterproof.

- Make it rugged.

- Make the footprint small.

In addition to the stamp, here is what you will need:

- Waterproof container

- Resealable plastic bags

- Logbook

- Ink pad (optional)

- Letterboxing info sheet

The Container

Heavy-duty freezer storage containers such as those made by Rubbermaid, Tupperware, and Lock & Lock seem to work well, if you make sure you use rugged ones with well-sealing lids. Any similar container will work, but avoid the lightweight "sandwich boxes" and cheap imitations; they don't seem to stand up to the elements as well. Look for something that is rugged and solid. The lids of flimsy containers can warp and crack from the elements, causing the boxes to take on water. Use a clear container so people can see its contents without opening it.

Keeping the container as small as possible is important: Using a smaller container increases the number of good hiding places and reduces the chance of accidental discovery. I most often use containers that are no larger than one and a half pints, unless I know beforehand that the hiding place will support a larger container.

Other good containers are Nalgene water bottles, the element-resistant containers used in scientific field research, and double-packed freezer storage containers. They offer better waterproofing, but are larger and more expensive. Do not use glass or any breakable material.

For the resealable bags, choose the heavy-duty ones over the wimpy sandwich bags, which tear more easily. Use the smallest size possible.

The Logbook

As with the personal logbook, your letterbox logbook should be unruled. Small spiral-bound sketchbooks work well. Many letterboxers have taken to making their own logbooks; these can add to a box's character, but they sometimes have fewer pages and can be less durable than store-bought sketchbooks. Use the smallest logbook you can find, but assume the pages

TIP It is generally better to get a smaller logbook, or cut a larger one down to size, than it is to get a bigger container to fit a large logbook.

need to be at least 2 by 2 inches to accommodate most signature stamps.

Waterproof paper is available for making logbooks, but water-based ink tends to smear on it. Use of this material is rarely seen in letterboxes.

You should include the name of your letterbox in the logbook (or elsewhere in the box or on it), so that it will not get confused with any other boxes or geocaches that may be in the area, and so that finders can look it up on the Internet in case there is a problem with it, or in case it is accidently found.

The Ink Pad

Some letterboxers, mostly in the Northeast, include an ink pad in their boxes. This is unnecessary, as all letterboxers carry their own with them. The benefits of providing an ink pad are that you can suggest which colors were intended for your stamp and attempt to ensure that your stamp is always inked with the same ink. The drawbacks are that it may increase box size or limit what else can be put in it (for example, "hitchhikers," a special box within the letterbox; see Chapter 7), they sometimes dry out, and if water gets in the box, it may lead to an inky mess. I recommend against putting an ink pad in your box.

Letterboxing Info Sheet

Include information about letterboxing in your box so that some-one who discovers it accidentally will know what it is and will leave it alone, or perhaps even join the pastime. At the very least, it is important to provide the name of the box and the website it is listed on, to facilitate contacting the placer. Examples are available on the primary letterboxing websites. I prefer some-thing much more concise, which I print out on a small sheet of paper and waterproof with packing tape:

This Is A letterbox, named Two Hens, listed on www.letterboxing.org

This box is part of a national treasure-hunting game called letterboxing. Please do not disturb it, and leave it exactly as you found it.

You are invited to participate in this pastime. For more information see www.letterboxing.org or www.atlasquest.com.

Packing It Up

Put the stamp in one resealable plastic bag. Put everything else in another. This will keep the ink on the stamp from getting all over the logbook. Pack everything in the container as tightly as possible. On the outside of the box, using a waterproof marker, indicate that it is a letterbox, not a geocache, and that it should not be disturbed.

Make sure you wash your hands well before assembling and placing a letterbox. Food scents that get transferred to the box may attract animals, which have been known to drag them away.

Some letterboxers like to include other items in their boxes, particularly self-addressed postcards, which allow them to receive a notification of who has found their box, and that it is still in good shape. This is fine for artistic purposes, but post-cards can get wet, and the advent of Internet logging of finds makes it unnecessary.

Basics of Rubber Stamp Artistry

In the early days of American letterboxing, most boxes contained store-bought stamps. Now, however, the store-bought stamp is becoming a thing of the past, and the stamp art in and of itself is becoming the reason to seek out certain boxes. Although there's no denying that it takes a degree of artistic talent to create the most sought-after stamps, creating basic rubber stamp art is a skill most people can master. With a little practice, you can become quite pleased with your work.

There are five considerations to creating a rubber stamp:

Robin's Nest is another fine example of why most letterboxers prefer to find hand-carved stamps.

- Artwork

- Carving media

- Transference method

- Carving tools and techniques

- Wood mounting (optional)

THE CARVING PROCESS

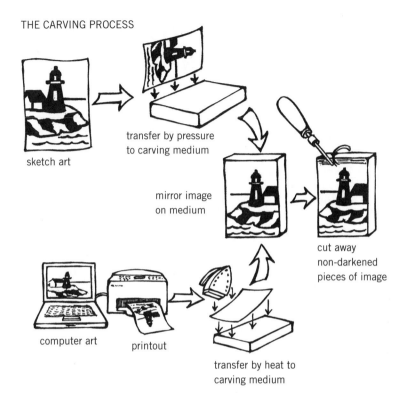

sketch art

transfer by pressure
to carving medium

mirror image
on medium

cut away
non-darkened
pieces of image

computer art

printout

transfer by heat to
carving medium

Whether the artwork used is a pencil sketch or computer-drawn art, first you
must transfer the image to the carving medium. Then you can carve away the
background, leaving the image in relief.

The basic idea is that you create or obtain artwork, either as
a sketch or using a computer drawing program, transfer it to the
carving medium, then carve away the material that is not part of

the transferred image. Then, if necessary or desired, add wood mounting to the medium.

Here is typically what you'll need:

- Sketchbook (if creating your own art)
- Iron or nail polish remover (for transference)
- Linoleum cutting set, craft knife, or scalpel
- Carving block or eraser
- Tweezers
- Wood backing (optional)
- Glue (optional)
- Sandpaper (optional)
- Lacquer (optional)

ARTWORK

The best letterboxing stamp art is original artwork that relates to or depicts the place, wildlife, or other aspect of the area where the box is hidden, or relates in some ways to the clues. For example, if the box is hidden near a historic building or in an area famous for a particular type of rare bird, renderings of these subjects would make good stamps.

One alternative is to sketch the image on acid-free sketch paper using a soft-leaded pencil. Keep in mind that the more detail you draw, the more skill it will take to carve it later. The darker you can draw the image, the easier it will be to transfer it to the carving medium.

Another option is to draw the image using a computer drawing program, or to use

BRIDGES OF LANCASTER

The Bridges of Lancaster is a perfect example of stamp art relating to the place—in this case, Lancaster County, Pennsylvania.

TIP The artwork doesn't have to be elaborate or complex. These paw-print stamps demonstrate uncomplicated stamp images, which, as a bonus, have educational value as well.

These stamps, known as The Paw Print Series, also depict the idea of a themed series of boxes.

BASICS OF RUBBER STAMP ARTISTRY

> **TIP** If using original computer art, draw it in black and white. If using clip art, try to find black-and-white images. If the art you want to use is in color, use the "convert to grayscale" function of your drawing program or print it in black and white. High-contrast images are more desirable, as sharp black-and-white images transfer better. If you have a color printer, you may need to configure it for black and white printing only.
>
> **TIP** If you are handy with a camera and a computer, a good source of original art is photographs you take. Upload or scan them into your image-editing software, and edit them a bit to simplify them.

clip art from one of many websites, some of which freely allow use of their clip art for noncommercial purposes. After printing the image on a laser printer, you can transfer it to the carving medium using an iron or nail polish remover.

When obtaining artwork from the Internet or elsewhere, make sure it is in the public domain or that its copyright or license agreement allows you to use it for this purpose.

To me, the most wonderful stamps tend to be those on which most of the medium is carved away, leaving the lines of your image. There are, however, some nice stamps that have been created by cutting the lines of the image into the medium.

Stamps in which most of the medium has been carved away (right) tend to make better images.

THE LETTERBOXER'S COMPANION

CARVING MEDIA

Your main choices for carving media are erasers and carving material made specifically for the purpose of creating hand-made rubber stamps. The three things to consider when choosing a medium are size, consistency, and thickness. Choice of a medium is a matter of personal taste and is often dictated by the size of the letterbox or the size and complexity of the artwork.

Carving media come in all sizes, thicknesses, and consistencies.

TIP Cut the carving media down to the size of your image. You don't want to leave a lot of blank area around the edges. Use a ruler or straightedge to guide your knife to get a straight, clean cut.

Size

Although it's nice to have a large stamp with a large image, trying to keep the box small often dictates a small stamp. Most erasers are small and do not need to be cut; most carving media can be cut to exact size.

Consistency

Don't use a medium that is too soft or crumbly, as is the case with some erasers. Most carving media are fine in this regard, though the consistency will vary somewhat from one to the next. Consistency will have an effect on how easy it is to carve detail. Softer materials are also more likely to require a wood mounting.

Thickness

A thick medium typically doesn't need a wood mounting; a thin stamp usually does if it is big enough. Most erasers are thick enough to hold up without a wood mounting. Carving media vary in thickness. Thinner media obviously take up less space.

Commonly Used Media

The following products work well for creating rubber stamps. Many can be found at arts and crafts stores; some must be ordered over the Internet. This is by no means a comprehensive list.

- *Stampeaz PZ Kut Carving Block* comes in 10-by-$4^3/_4$-inch sheets, $^1/_4$ inch thick. This is the choice of many carving enthusiasts. It can be cut to the size you need, but because of its thinness, all but the smallest stamps will need to be mounted. Softer than erasers and good for detail, it's available on the Internet (for the web address see "Internet Resources" at the end of this book).

- *Speedball Speedy-Stamp Carving Block* comes in 4-by-6-inch sheets, among other sizes, and is $1/4$ inch thick. Affectionately known as the "pink stuff," it typically needs to be wood mounted. Be careful not to get Speedball's white medium, which doesn't work nearly as well.

- *Staedtler Mastercarve Artist Carving Block* comes in different sizes, and is $3/4$ inch thick. It is somewhat soft and good for detail, and its thickness means you may not need a wood mounting for all carvings.

- *Staedtler Mars Plastic Eraser,* $2^1/2$ by $3/4$ by $1/2$ inch, is a hard, easy-to-carve medium. Because of its hardness and dimensions, you will not need a wood mounting. Staedtler also makes a larger size, which is harder to find. One disadvantage of this product is that one side has a raised logo and the other side has inked writing that has to be removed.

- *Factis Plastic Eraser,* $2^7/8$ by $1^1/2$ by $1/2$ inch, is a little softer than the Staedtler Mars, but still easy to carve. You will typically not need a wood mounting. This is a good choice for beginners. Its relatively large size offers a lot of space to work with, yet it is not so large that it needs to be cut. Be sure to get the one in the blue wrapper. Factis also makes other erasers; the one you commonly see in the orange wrapper is smaller and too soft.

TRANSFERENCE METHOD

Unless you carve or draw your artwork directly into the medium, which some master carvers do, you will need to transfer the image before carving it out. There are a few ways to do this, depending on whether your art is a pencil sketch or a computer printout or photocopy.

Pencil Sketch Art

If you are using sketch art as your source, draw it as dark as possible with a soft lead pencil on sketch paper. Place the sketch on a flat surface, then press the medium onto the sketch as firmly as possible, being careful to keep it steady. The mirror image of your art will now be on the medium. Darken or fill in any missing parts of the artwork with your pencil; then carve out the parts that are not dark.

TIP You will be transferring the mirror image onto the medium so it comes out correctly when stamped. If you are carving or drawing directly onto the medium, remember to draw numbers and letters in reverse.

Using Tracing Paper

This method is similar in principle to using sketch art, except that you will be tracing an image from another source, such as a computer printout or photocopy, rather than drawing an image from scratch on sketch paper.

You trace the image onto tracing paper using a soft-lead pencil, and then transfer the pencil lead to the carving medium. Place the tracing paper over the image, and trace as much detail as you would like in your final image. Make sure you keep your pencil sharp (or use a mechanical pencil), and keep your lines sharp and consistent. You may wish to tape the paper over the image to keep it steady. When satisfied with your tracing, press the paper as hard and as evenly as possible onto the medium to transfer the lead, being careful to keep it steady. As with the other methods, the mirror image of your art will now be on the medium. Darken or fill in any missing parts of the artwork with your pencil, and carve out the parts that are not dark.

Using an Iron

If your art is a computer printout or photocopy from a laser printer or toner-based copier, you can use heat to transfer the toner to the medium. This method will not work with printouts from ink-jet printers. Set the iron on its lowest non-steam setting. Place the medium on the ironing board; then place the image printed side down against the medium. Press the iron firmly onto the back of the paper (avoid the holes on the iron's soleplate). If the medium is not perfectly flat, you may need to rock the iron back and forth a bit. Keep the heat and pressure applied for about thirty seconds; then remove the paper quickly. (Irons and media vary; you'll have to experiment with this to keep the paper from sticking to the medium.) You may need to touch up by hand parts of the image that did not get transferred before carving out the parts that are not dark.

Using Acetone

Acetone is a chemical found in nail polish remover. If your source art is a computer printout or photocopy from a laser printer or toner-based copier, you can use acetone to transfer toner to the medium. This method will not work with printouts from ink-jet printers. Place the image printed side down against the medium. Wet a tissue or cotton ball with acetone, firmly rub the back of the paper for a few seconds, and then remove the paper quickly. Carve out the parts that are not dark. You may need to touch up by hand parts of the image that did not get transferred.

Caution: Acetone is a dangerous, extremely flammable chemical. Read the directions and cautions on the bottle before using. Do not experiment with acetone and heat transference at the same time or on the same piece of carving material.

Using Transparency Film

The toner transference methods described above won't work with ink-jet printers. One way to transfer ink from ink-jet printers is to print the images on transparency film. Use the film specifically made for ink-jet printers (as opposed to laser printers). Print the image on the smooth side of the film so that it won't dry (the opposite of what the film's instructions say). Let it sit for a few minutes and then very carefully, against a hard, flat surface like a tabletop, press the medium to the printed image. This works best if your image is gray rather than black, as too much ink for this purpose is used when printing black images. You will have to play with this a bit to get it to work well for your particular ink and printer, but once you get it right, it works well.

CARVING TOOLS AND TECHNIQUES

For carving tools, you will need a craft knife (such as an X-Acto), a scalpel, or a cutting set like the Speedball linoleum cutters. This set comes with a handle and five or six interchangeable cutting blades called nibs. Beginners generally find the Speedball set easier to get started with, while many veteran rubber stamp artists seem to prefer the X-Acto knife. It is often handy to have both on hand. It may be helpful to have tweezers and a magnifying glass as well. Set up a comfortable, well-lit work area. Have the original artwork on hand to refer to, even if the image has been transferred onto the medium.

Stamp carving involves cutting away the parts of the rubber that are not inked in the transference process, leaving the inked parts raised as your stamp image. I find it best to do the most detailed parts first. If using the Speedball system, use the #1 nib, cut around the general outline of the main components of the image, following the line where toner or lead meets the blank medium, and then work on the detailed areas. When you are satisfied with the detailed areas, use a larger nib such as a #3 to cut out the bigger blank areas; then use the #1 nib for touch-ups.

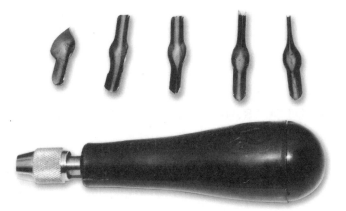

The Speedball carving set is a good choice for beginners.

THE LETTERBOXER'S COMPANION

ANGLED-AWAY VERSUS ANGLED-IN CARVING

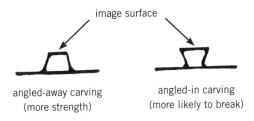

image surface

angled-away carving
(more strength)

angled-in carving
(more likely to break)

You can guard against the medium breaking with angled-away carving (left).

Cut away from the most detailed areas toward the blank areas. It is easier to start the blade exactly where you want it than to stop exactly where you should. Also, a slip of the hand along the way will be less likely to damage the parts of the image you have already carved.

If you won't be using a wood mounting, you will typically need to cut about $1/16$ to $1/8$ inch deep, depending on the consistency and strength of the rubber. You can get away with shallower cutting if you intend to mount the stamp, or if you cut away all the excess medium that surrounds the image. You don't need to cut deeply in particularly detailed areas, especially if there is a lot of surrounding image to provide support, or if you leave a border on your stamp.

Caution: Carving tools are sharp. Always cut away from your hands and body, and don't hold the stamp so that the momentum from a slip of the hand will carry the tool toward the hand holding the stamp.

WOOD MOUNTING

Once you have a finished stamp, you'll have to decide if you want or need a wood mounting. Thinner, softer stamps will need it for support, or you may wish to add it for artistic effect. A mounting makes the stamp bigger, however, possibly increasing the footprint of the box, and it adds time and expense to the project for something you will be leaving out in the woods, so it is completely optional. If you're not sure, it is usually better to go with the mounting, as wood-mounted stamps often give better images because of the added support.

Use thin plywood or other suitable thin wood, around $3/8$ inch thick. Measure the stamp and add $1/8$ to $1/4$ inch all around. Cut the wood to size; then sand it down with fine-grain sandpaper, roughing up the side that will be glued to the rubber. Stamp the side that will not be attached to the rubber with the stamp image, if you'd like.

Cut small gouges or lines in the back of the rubber (the side that will be attached to the wood). Apply a thin, even layer of waterproof, temperature-resistant household adhesive to glue the rubber to the wood.

Let the adhesive set according to the manufacturer's instructions (typically overnight). Some people seal the wood with lacquer for an even more professional look.

> **TIP** Apply the glue as even and as flat as possible, so the rubber mounts flat on the wood.

Letterboxing Etiquette and Conventions

It has been said many times that the only rule is that there are no rules, and this is certainly true of the pastime of letterboxing in terms of the creative aspects, such as clever hiding methods and innovative clues. The variations and innovations in clues, hiding places, and stamps, as well as other interesting elements of the pastime, can be mind-boggling. However, there are some conventions, etiquette, and other guidelines you should be aware of.

Despite its sometimes solitary nature and sometimes shroud of secrecy, letterboxing is really a community activity. By looking out for each other's boxes and respecting a few common-sense guidelines, everyone's enjoyment is enhanced. Moreover, the careless or inconsiderate activities of one letterboxer can reflect badly on everyone in the hobby, cause authorities to take a dim view of it and ban it in their parks, and be a sure ticket to getting booted out of the letterboxing community.

LEAVE NO TRACE

Aside from the box, which should be placed without disturbing the environment (see Chapter 4, page 30), letterboxing is an "invisible" activity. Respect the land when hunting boxes and when hiding them. Don't place a box that requires people to tramp through sensitive wildlife or plant habitat to find it, and don't tear up an area when looking for a box. If you can't find the box without leaving the land as you found it, enjoy the hike and go look for another. If you have any doubts about an area, ask the landowner or manager, or choose another location for your activities. Some areas have restrictions on land use; know them and observe them.

Some important Leave No Trace principles to follow:

- *Know before you go.* Be prepared with clothing to protect you from cold, heat, or rain. Use maps to navigate so you won't get lost. Learn about the areas you visit—the more you know, the more you fun you'll have.

- *Choose the right path.* Stay on the main trail and don't wander far by yourself. Do not trample or cut flowers or small trees. Once disturbed, they might not grow back.

- *Trash your trash.* Pack it in, pack it out. Put litter, including crumbs, in trash cans or carry it home. Keep water clean. Do not put soap, food, or waste in lakes or streams.

- **Leave what you find.** Leave plants, rocks, and historical items as you find them so the next person can enjoy them.

- **Respect wildlife.** Observe animals from a distance and never approach, feed, or follow them. Human food is unhealthy for all animals, and feeding them starts bad habits. Protect wildlife by storing your meals and trash. Control pets at all times or leave them at home.

- **Be kind to other visitors.** Make sure not to bother others while enjoying the outdoors. Listen to nature. Avoid making loud noises or yelling. You will see more animals if you are quiet.

MONITORING YOUR BOXES

At the very minimum, you should monitor the boxes you place to make sure a social trail or other environmental impact hasn't developed. Make sure the contents are intact and dry, and make any necessary repairs. If the placement of a box has led to impact, or changes to the area have rendered the clues inaccurate, it should be removed, and notification of its removal should be made on the website where it is listed. Monitoring your boxes is fun: You can read the logbook to see who has stamped in, and once in a while you'll meet others on the trail who are seeking your box.

If your clues are listed on Atlas Quest, other AQ users may notify you that the box needs first aid, and you will be able to note on your clue page that the box is in need of repair, so perhaps someone else will fix it if you can't get to it. AQ also allows the option of comments on listed clues, which can be an effective way to keep track of any issues with the box or the clue. Both AQ and LbNA have "Contact the Placer" functions and ways to report finds and attempted finds; a drop-off in reported finds and an increase in attempts may be an indication that the box has gone missing and that you should go check it out.

You should update your clues on these websites when necessary. On Atlas Quest, you should note the fact that you checked the status of your box on the clue summary page, using the "Confirm Status" function, even if no changes or repairs were made.

MONITORING OTHERS' BOXES

Many letterboxers carry plastic resealable bags, spare logbooks, and other repair materials with them when they go out

TIP Most box owners like to be alerted if their boxes have gone missing, but you should have evidence that it is missing before making such a report. Boxes reported as missing are often still intact; in these cases, the seeker simply made a wrong turn or misinterpreted the clues. The convention on both AQ and LbNA is to mark the box as "attempted" if you think it has gone missing.

TIP While most box owners welcome constructive criticism, don't use the "Contact the Placer" function to whine about the box and make a general annoyance of yourself. If you didn't enjoy the box, the hike was not for you, or the clues were too hard or too easy, simply move on and find another letterbox.

on the hunt, in case they find a box in need of repair. It is a good idea for you to do so; the community has evolved into one where people look out for others' boxes. If a social trail is developing to a box you find, or the clues no longer work due to recent changes in the area, or the box needs repairs that you are unable to make, you should notify the person who placed it. Atlas Quest and LbNA provide "Contact the Placer" features for this purpose.

Both AQ and LbNA allow finds to be logged on boxes, and AQ allows comments (at the option of the owner) to be logged. This is one way to leave positive feedback that the box is fine.

SECRECY AND SPOILERS

Some letterboxers view the activity as shrouded in mystique and secrecy: sneaking around the woods, keeping quiet about the boxes they've found, using hidden clues, surprise twists, and so on. Most others are more open about their activities, and they enjoy discussing the details of their adventures on the trail and logging their finds and comments online.

Whichever mode of operation you prefer, never give or post spoilers or other information that could give away the solution to a clue or the location of a box. It's easy to talk too much, especially on the Internet. Clue writers often put a considerable amount of time into their puzzles, and posting spoilers is just plain rude. It also ruins the fun for the people who enjoy solving these puzzles.

> **TIP** Announcing that you solved a particularly difficult clue can be fun, but be careful in what you say and how you say it. For some clues (especially mysteries; see Chapter 7), it is easy to give away too much simply by the act of posting. When in doubt, silence is golden, and the mystique surrounding the box that you successfully cracked will continue to grow. While Atlas Quest has taken some steps to allow logging of finds of these boxes and still not give away the solution for others, it is all too easy to spill the beans yourself by posting on one of the forums. For example, if you post that you found boxes X, Y, and Z today, and Z is a difficult mystery box with an uncertain location, anyone can look up the locations of X and Y and get a general idea of the location of Z, spoiling the hard work of its creator.

Do not post stamp images on the Internet from boxes you have found without the permission of the person who created the stamp. Think of stamps as the property of the creator.

ADOPTION, ABANDONMENT, AND RETIREMENT

You should never abandon a letterbox you have placed. If you are no longer interested in keeping it active, you should "retire" it. (On Atlas Quest, it is preferable to retire it rather than delete it, so that it can remain in the database for virtual logbooks, counts, and such.) Alternatively, on Atlas Quest you can transfer it to another owner, provided you have their permission first and both owners have AQ accounts. Boxes listed on AQ may eventually be removed if they are not maintained.

If you encounter a letterbox you believe is abandoned, you should first attempt to contact the placer, either on AQ or LbNA, depending on where the box is listed. If you don't receive a response, it is possible that it has been abandoned. Atlas Quest does not permit adoption of abandoned letterboxes, but LbNA does, at the discretion of the webmasters. If you wish to adopt it, contact the LbNA webmasters. This is a good way to keep a particularly interesting box in circulation or to make sure it is maintained and not simply cluttering up the environment. If you do receive a response from the original placer, on Atlas Quest they may be willing to transfer ownership to you.

POACHING

Poaching is when you base the starting point of your clue on the location of someone else's box without asking them. Doing this without the permission of the owner of that box is annoying because sometimes this can give away the location of that box.

TRAIL NAMES

Most letterboxers take aliases or "trail names." This can be fun, especially when you find a clever way to relate the name to your signature stamp or to the style of boxes you hide. This is also the name you should use when creating an account on one of the letterboxing websites.

EXCHANGES

Sometimes you'll encounter other letterboxers on the trail or at gatherings. While a few purists observe the Dartmoor tradition that the signature stamp is not exchanged in person, it is otherwise customary to exchange signature stamp images with other letterboxers.

> **TIP** If you wish to keep your signature stamp secret yet still participate in exchanges, create and carry a traveler for this purpose (see Chapter 7). This is more in keeping with Dartmoor traditions and is becoming more popular in this country.

GATHERINGS

One of the most enjoyable aspects of letterboxing is the gathering. Besides meeting fun people to swap letterboxing stories around the fire with, gatherings almost always have the following three ingredients:

- An interesting place

- An event stamp

- "Day of" boxes

Special stamps are typically carved for gatherings.

Gatherings are usually organized by local letterboxers and take place at a park with plenty of boxes. These events can be held anywhere in the country. They are often potluck affairs that last the afternoon, or are held during dinner at restaurants or pubs.

Often a master carver is recruited to carve the event stamp, which can be obtained only by attending the gathering. (Often the stamp is not finalized until just before it is placed in a box at the end of the gathering.) These stamps are sometimes the most stunning works of art in letterboxing.

The organizer usually hides a few boxes that will be in place only on that day, or will be available for the first time that day. These can be fun, especially when the hunt is in a pub setting.

Times and locations of most gatherings are listed on Atlas Quest (where they are called "Events"), but occasionally the details of one will be buried in a clue or other mysterious post in a forum.

MINDING YOUR Ps AND Fs

Some letterboxers like to keep statistics on their activities, in particular their "PFX count," which is the number of boxes they've placed and found, and the exchanges they've made. For example, a PFX count of "P73 F188 X10"means this letterboxer has placed 73 boxes, found 188, and made 10 exchanges with other letterboxers. Letterboxing is not a competitive pastime, and some letterboxers roll their eyes when these numbers are mentioned, but many people like them, and they certainly can be viewed in a noncompetitive light. Track them or not, as you wish; all counting is done on the honor system, and there is no central agency that verifies these numbers. Some people have patches made for reaching certain milestones, and there are boxes that can be stamped once you reach 100 and 500 finds.

Atlas Quest automatically tracks your PFX count for traditional letterboxes, assuming that you log the boxes you've found on the website. The caveat is that you must be a premium member of the site to log finds of boxes not listed on the site. In the early days there was controversy over whether or not to include "hitchhikers" (see Chapter 7), event (gathering) stamps, and other non-ordinary stamps and boxes in these counts, but Atlas Quest simply breaks these statistics out separately. Atlas Quest displays trophies and ribbons on your profile for reaching certain milestones, and provides a Hall of Fame as well.

Many people don't use Atlas Quest to log their finds; in fact, the person with the most at the time of writing wasn't even listed there, and some count differently than Atlas Quest does. This has become an unimportant issue in the letterboxing world to many (in fact, boasting about large PFX counts has come to be viewed by many as a negative), as it is better to be known for your deeds. I thought I'd at least mention the PFX count, though, as it gives an immediate perspective on how active a letterboxer is (or was).

Advanced Techniques

Since letterboxing was introduced to America, many clever ideas have been invented or borrowed from Dartmoor, both in the creation and placement of boxes, and in the writing of clues. This chapter contains a sampling of some of the more fun and devious things you may discover on the trail of a letterbox. Intentionally incomplete so

Flutterby

The famous *Flutterby*, the box that finds you, is just one example of the innovative ideas that have come along.

as not to spoil the thrill of discovery, the information is provided simply to explain some of the more common terms and techniques you may see and to spur your imagination.

MICRO BOXES

Micro boxes, as the name implies, are very small letterboxes. These boxes open up the possibility of more clever and devious hiding places, and make it easier to prevent accidental discovery. They can be almost impossible to find without precise solving of the clues, and, despite their size, can be constructed to offer a surprisingly large stamp and logbook. The container typically used is a 35mm film canister.

To build a micro box, here is what you'll need:

- 35mm film canister with lid

- Thin carving medium (such as Speedball's Speedy-Stamp Carving Block)

- Scroll paper

- Duct tape or equivalent

- Hook-and-loop tape (such as Velcro)

Micro boxes are sometimes created using scroll paper, folding stamps, and old film canisters.

The Stamp

The stamp can be a single piece or in several pieces, though typically it's not more than two. For a single stamp, assuming a medium the thickness of the Speedy-Stamp Carving Block, cut a piece no bigger than 1 by $1^5/_8$ inches (the height of the container).

You can include a bigger stamp by folding it. Cut a piece of block no bigger than $1^7/_8$ by $1^5/_8$ inches. Carve your stamp image; then cut down the middle of the front of the image, but not all the way through. Leave the two halves attached by a thin amount of carving block so it folds, and then back it with strong, weather-resistant tape. You should be able to fold the stamp so it fits in the canister, and unfold it to stamp up, with the seam barely noticeable, if at all.

This is *The Inventor* micro box stamp, shown actual size.

The Logbook

You will need some sort of paper that can be rolled up like a scroll. The width of your paper will be the height of the canister, and it can be as long as will fit rolled up and still leave room for your stamp. You can also use paper that's twice as wide (about 3 inches), and fold it lengthwise before rolling it up. Write a short "What Is Letterboxing?" note at the top, roll it up so it fits along

> **TIP** For a larger logbook, try to find thin paper that is about 3 feet long. One thing that works, and that's already in a natural scroll shape, is cash register tape, available at office supply stores.

the inside wall of the canister, and then put your stamp in the middle.

The Hiding Place

You can put micro boxes in interesting places using hook-and-loop tape (Velcro)—assuming you have permission, of course. Use the industrial strength, waterproof, self-adhesive sheets that are 2 inches wide. Wrap the fuzzy sheet around the canister, and attach the hard sheet where you want to attach the box.

> **TIP** Some people have used magnets, such as the small round ones you can get at arts and crafts stores, to attach micro boxes to metallic objects, such as park benches and signposts, found in urban settings.

HITCHHIKERS

Hitchhikers (often called "movers" or "parasites" in Dartmoor), are boxes that live in other letterboxes and are moved from box to box as people find them. They do not have clues and usually do not have a physical box; they are typically just a stamp and logbook in a plastic bag. Hitchhikers are completely separate from their host box or "hostel."

When you find a hitchhiker, you stamp its logbook with your signature stamp, then stamp your logbook with its stamp just like any other box. When you place a hitchhiker in another box, you stamp that box's logbook with the hitchhiker's stamp, and stamp the hitchhiker's logbook with the hostel box's stamp.

This stamp, the World Domination Hitchhiker, travels from one letterbox to the next.

If you find a hitchhiker, there is no requirement that you take it, but if you do, you should make every effort to place it in another box within a month to keep it in circulation. You may place it in any box that is large enough to hold it.

It is generally considered acceptable etiquette to disclose where you've found a hitchhiker, but bad etiquette to disclose where you've placed one. Note, however, that some hitchhikers have specific instructions that differ from this general rule.

Sometimes hitchhikers do have their own box, and may be placed outside their hostel in the same hiding place.

TIP Make sure your hitchhiker's container and logbook are labeled as such, so they are not confused with the contents of the host box, which may not be labeled at all.

ADVANCED TECHNIQUES

MYSTERY BOXES

Mystery boxes are boxes whose clues have a vague or unknown starting location. Most clues give you clear directions to where to start the hunt; mystery boxes are the exact opposite. They are usually presented as a story or as a cryptic puzzle, and you have to figure out where to begin. Sometimes you don't even know the state a box is hidden in; for others you are at least given the region, state, or county.

An example might be a story set at the site of a Revolutionary War battle, with a description of the battle as the background of the story. The first step might be to figure out that it was a Revolutionary War battle, then determine which battle and where it was fought. From that place you then begin solving the rest of the puzzle. Other examples include hidden words or other wordplay, giving the text a double meaning, or the clues might weave in local folklore or legend. Mystery boxes are often the most challenging and rewarding of finds.

Note that it is considered bad etiquette to post or discuss the fact that you have found a particular mystery box if doing so will give away its general location. You can still log these finds on Atlas Quest, however, as its logging feature is set up so that it won't spoil the clue.

CUCKOO CLUES

A cuckoo clue is a normal clue to a letterbox that is not published anywhere, but travels from one letterbox to another, like a hitchhiker. Cuckoo clues typically have an attached log sheet where you stamp your signature stamp and the stamp from the box you place the clue in. When you find a cuckoo clue, you copy it to use later, then send it on its way in another box for others to find.

It is generally considered bad etiquette to discuss cuckoo clues that you find, and to discuss hidden clues in general. If you are creating a cuckoo clue, you should identify it as such, and provide brief instructions on how it works, for the benefit of others who may not have seen one before.

WoM CLUES AND HIDDEN CLUES

WoM clues are unpublished clues passed by word of mouth. There are also many devious ways to hide letterbox clues just about anywhere, such as on letterboxers' personal websites, concealed in idle chatter on an Internet talk list, or in a book about letterboxing. Be alert and you may discover one somewhere! If you create a WoM clue, make sure to identify it as such, and include any restrictions or instructions regarding how it may be passed on.

DISTRIBUTED CLUES

Sometimes clues are distributed in parts that have to be put together like a jigsaw puzzle. Parts of clues can be carved into stamp images, either as words or as pictures (in other words, a rebus). For example, if you have a ten-word clue, you could carve

Distributed pictorial clues are rebus-like. Left to right from top to bottom: Appalachian Trail, Round Bald top (summit), 70 degrees, 25 paces, and boulder.

two words into each of five stamps, then hide them in five different boxes. Seekers would have to find all five, and then figure out the order to put them in to get the ten-word clue to the box. Instead of words, clever pictures could accomplish the same effect.

BONUS BOXES AND ADD-ONS

A bonus box is a clue to another box hidden in a letterbox; typically it is an extension of the hunt for the box it is found in, and it is often found in the last box of a series. Unlike a cuckoo clue, the clue to a bonus box is not removed from the box it is found in.

Adding on (or "poaching") is when you add clues to someone else's box that lead to your own box, as in "starting at box X, follow the red trail"; that is, the clues to your box use the other box as a starting point. The clues are usually published, but they can be placed as a bonus box in the other person's box. It is considered bad etiquette to add on to or poach someone else's box without their permission.

> **TIP** When creating an add-on box (assuming you have the owner's permission) and publishing the clues, be careful that your clues don't give away the location of the other person's box. If you're not careful, it can be easy for someone to find the add-on box and work backward to the other box.

TRAVELERS

Travelers (often called "personal travelers") are sometimes confused with hitchhikers, but they are completely different. A traveler is a stamp a letterboxer carries for exchanging images with other letterboxers met on the trail. There is usually a secret code that must be said, or some other action that must be performed, to gain access to someone's traveler. Travelers are sometimes carried so the letterboxer can keep his or her signature stamp a secret and still participate in exchanges.

MULTIPART STAMPS

It can be fun to carve a large stamp image and cut it into pieces, hiding each piece in a different letterbox. Typically, this is done in a single series of letterboxes, but it doesn't have to be. The seeker then has to find each box to get the complete image.

LETTERBOOKS AND HIPS BOXES

A letterbook is a hollowed-out book that is used as the container for a letterbox. The stamp and logbook are placed in the hollowed-out section, and the book is usually placed in a library or bookstore (with the owner's permission, of course). A letterbook is an example of a "hidden in plain sight" (HIPS) letterbox, in which ordinary visible objects are actually letterboxes in disguise. The possibilities here are endless, especially in a pub or other indoor setting or at a gathering.

COOTIES AND FLEAS

Cooties are small letterboxes that are hidden on other people or in their gear without their knowledge. It is usually just a stamp and sometimes a small logbook. If you later discover you have caught a cootie (usually at a gathering), you stamp in, and then try to foist it onto another letterboxer as soon as possible. A flea is a cootie that can also be placed in another letterbox like a hitchhiker.

ANAGRAMS, ACROSTICS, AND OTHER WORDPLAY

An *anagram* is formed by rearranging the letters of a word or phrase to spell another word or phrase. Anagrams are a fun technique to use when writing clues, and something to look out for when you encounter a clue you can't otherwise make sense of.

For example, a clue might contain the instruction "Look for where the 'eighth soul' stands watch." This might not make sense at first, but realizing that the letters that spell "eighth soul" can be rearranged into "house light" or "lighthouse" may shed some light on the issue, depending on the rest of the clue or the location.

As a harder example, a clue may be titled "The Unholy Madrigals." Unless what follows in the clue is a series of madrigals that seems to lead to a letterbox, it may pay to work the title as an anagram by transposing the letters until you come up with a new word or phrase. Give up? The answer is "Maryland Lighthouse."

An *acrostic* uses the first letter of each word, phrase, or sentence in a series to spell another word or phrase. This technique can be used in clues as a clever way to give instructions, or by the seeker to make sense of apparently meaningless prose or verse. A clue can also be written as a series of trivia questions, with the first letter of each answer spelling a phrase that really describes where the letterbox is hidden, or provides a hint as to how to unravel the remaining clues.

Sample acrostic:

- State named for wife of King Charles I

- Old Irish alphabetic system

- Tortola, Danish West Indies, et al.

- Country with the world's oldest surviving parliament

- Country whose capital is Tallinn

In this case, the answers to the trivia questions are "Maryland," "Ogham," "Virgin Islands," "Iceland," and "Estonia." Thus the solution to the acrostic is the word "movie." This clue is a hint telling you that a film somehow plays a role in unraveling the mystery. Perhaps you'll need to be on the lookout for the name of a film or for where a particular film was shot. Which movie, or other details, may be specified in other parts of the clue. The remaining clues might be written in a more straightforward and direct way or in the form of an even longer acrostic. With a longer one, the entire directions to a letterbox could be spelled out this way. As things like acrostics have become more common, clue writers have taken to using the last letter of words rather than the first, and so forth, so be on the lookout.

A *rebus* is a phrase represented by images or symbols whose sounds correspond with the sounds of syllables in the phrase. The example of distributed pictorial clues on page 86 is rebus-like. The pictures and symbols can be interpreted as phrases or clues. In particular, the ball plus the "D" that forms "bald," and the bowl plus the "DR" that forms "boulder" are typical of rebuses. The possibilities are endless.

These methods are a small sampling of letterboxing word-play. Countless other word puzzle techniques can be woven into clues.

BOOK CODES

A book code can be a fun way to write clues, and in reality, some famous codes in history have been done this way, so it can give your clue a historical or treasure-hunting feel. Top it off by making it part of the puzzle to figure out which book is being used, or that it is even a book code in the first place, and these puzzle clues can become quite elaborate.

There are many ways to do this, but the basic idea is simple: Give a page or chapter number, followed by a word number on that page or in that chapter. By assembling the words in the order specified, a message is spelled out. For example, the following code uses words from this book; the first number in each pair is the page number, and the second is the word number on that page:

17-8   3-13   23-7   85-69   12-5   1-11   12-12
4-39   48-38   26-8   11-63

> **TIP** When creating or solving book codes, you must be certain to specify the edition of the book in question, or be sure you have the correct one. Also, the text doesn't have to be a true book; it can be any well-known or famous text, or text from a web page.

OTHER CODES AND CIPHERS

One of the most basic types of ciphers is the cryptogram, a simple letter-substitution cipher where, for example, every "A" becomes a "T," every "B" an "H," every "C" an "E," and so forth. The idea is to puzzle it out, or perhaps the key to the cipher is hidden in another part of the clue, or it is a famous cipher from history, requiring the solver to do the research. Give this simple cryptogram a try:

VKMY ABC LDQDMSCY GHSF KM AGHPWB
SGCCF XADAC TDGF VHQQHI ABC MHGAB
LHPMY AGDKQ AH D UPMSAKHM

This, and many more sophisticated codes and ciphers, can be found in the more advanced letterboxing clues, and many people find these sorts of clues more interesting. Find an obscure cipher to encrypt your clues, or create your own. Below is an example of the famous Freemason's cipher (or "pigpen cipher"), which has been used throughout history and has appeared in letterboxing clues to give them an interesting visual appeal. Research this famous cipher on the Internet, and give it a try:

INTERNET DATABASES

When constructing or solving the clues for particularly difficult boxes, think about using government databases on the Internet. One of the most useful, especially for locating obscure geographical features (such as "Round Bald" in the pictorial clues on page 86), is the Geographic Names Information System (GNIS), which can be located at http://geonames.usgs.gov. Google Maps (http://maps.google.com) and similar sites can also be used to locate these features. See "Internet Resources" at the end of the book for additional help.

VISUAL CLUES

Some clues are given solely as a series of pictures or artwork that you have to follow, and some are presented as antique-looking treasure maps. Props like these add a certain charm to the hunt.

GPS

A GPS (Global Positioning System) device allows you to pinpoint a location anywhere on Earth to within about 15 feet, using a set of coordinates. It also can be used to tell you how far you are from a given point (called a waypoint).

Clues can be given simply as a waypoint, or as a distance from several waypoints, or as a puzzle whose answer is a waypoint. Some clues give you three waypoints and the distance from them, requiring you to determine a fourth waypoint to visit, and so forth. Many letterboxers do not own GPS units or

GPS-enabled devices, or don't particularly like waypoints in clues, but there is no reason you can't use them; in fact, some of the first letterboxes placed were based on GPS coordinates.

If you encounter GPS coordinates in clues, keep in mind that you can often find the box without using a GPS unit, and this can be quite fun. Websites such as http://store.usgs.gov will allow you to navigate to the coordinates on a locator map and download a topographical map, which you can use along with other information in the clue. You can also purchase print copies of these U.S. Geological Survey (USGS) maps at many outdoor outfitters. Using these maps, you find waypoints with traditional map and compass navigational techniques.

The hobby of geocaching, which is in some ways similar to letterboxing, caters more to GPS enthusiasts. For more information on geocaching, see *The Geocaching Handbook* (Falcon-Guides) or www.geocaching.com.

If you are using GPS or a compass app on a smartphone, make sure you are aware of the technical differences from the real thing in both creating and solving clues.

VIRTUAL LETTERBOXES

Virtual letterboxes are clues that you solve on a website. They aren't actually letterboxes but are more like online puzzles that may or may not require you to visit real-world locations to find the answers.

CHRISTMAS BOXES

Themed boxes relating to a particular holiday, or boxes that will be out for only a short while, can be fun. These sorts of boxes add a "limited edition" feel.

GHOST TOWNS AND CRASH SITES

Hunting for ghost towns, aircraft crash sites, and the like are hobbies in their own right, but these hobbies can offer a splendid combination with letterboxing. The puzzle of finding these locations, laid down by time and history, can be woven into a letterbox clue, often as a story, usually as a mystery box. Some clues along these lines already exist, and there are many exciting possibilities for further development of this advanced style of clue.

OUT-OF-THE-BOX THINKING

There are countless types of letterboxes. Some boxes find you; others are always moving around. You might find a box that allows you to move it and modify its clues. Another box could require you to watch a movie, figure out where a particular scene was shot, and then, based on clues in the scene, go there and find the box (for example, "Find where Kate Whitney's car goes off a cliff."). The possibilities are endless.

FINAL THOUGHTS

Whether you enjoy playing with the advanced techniques discussed in this chapter to write cryptic treasure hunts, or prefer writing straightforward directions to that special place; whether you enjoy solving mind-bending puzzles or prefer taking a casual hike for a sought-after stamp—you'll experience the thrill of discovery in this fast-growing yet quaint pastime.

Letterboxing has something for everyone. This intriguing mix of hiking, rubber stamp artistry, and problem solving appeals to people of all ages, backgrounds, and interests. This activity is being enjoyed by individuals, families, and teams. While this book aims to give you the basic information you need to participate (and a few interesting advanced techniques), my best advice is to grab some clues, hit the trail, and experience it for yourself.

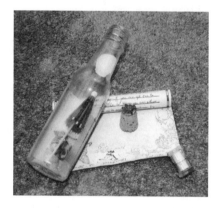

You never know what curiosities you'll find out there, like this message in a bottle with a micro hitchhiker.

Internet Resources

This chapter describes some websites that are useful to the beginning and experienced letterboxer alike.

LETTERBOXING CLUE WEBSITES

Atlas Quest (www.atlasquest.com)

Since the publication of the first edition of this book, Atlas Quest (commonly known as AQ) has become the dominant letterboxing website. At the time of writing, AQ claims about 57,000 active traditional letterboxes and about 25,000 registered members.

Aside from its clue database, AQ is rich with tutorials on all aspects of letterboxing, member forums, tools to manage and report on boxes, and sophisticated search tools (i.e., aside from searching for clues to boxes near a given city or zip code, you can search for boxes within a given geographic rectangle or along a geographic line).

Anyone can search for letterbox clues on the site, but you must become a registered member to post letterbox clues and post to the forums. Registration for these uses (and most others) is free; however, there is a premium membership available that is required for a handful of features, such as downloading clues to a mobile device.

Finding clues near you on AQ is simple. Just enter your zip code in the "Location-Based Search" box on the main page, and a list of clues is returned. Posting clues is more involved, as there is a myriad of options, but a six-step wizard guides you through the process.

AQ allows registered members to log finds and attempts, and to comment on boxes listed on AQ (premium members may also log finds of boxes not listed on AQ), though the creator of the box may restrict how these logs are displayed.

AQ has a restriction system that allows planters to restrict who can see their clues. Clues can be restricted by number of finds logged, number of plants, or AQ group membership. For example, planters may require that you have one hundred logged AQ finds before their clues become available to you.

AQ is a rich, complex beast, and it takes quite a while to learn all of its features. However, the basics for the new letter-boxer are straightforward.

Letterboxing North America (www.letterboxing.org)

Letterboxing North America (commonly known as LbNA), is the oldest post-*Smithsonian*–era letterboxing website, with its origins dating back to 1998. At the time of writing, LbNA lists a total of about 38,000 boxes and about 12,000 active members.

As with AQ, anyone can search for letterbox clues on the site, but you must become a registered member to post clues. Membership is free, though donations to defray the cost of operating the site are accepted.

Finding clues near you is less sophisticated than on AQ; the best way is to click on "Search for Boxes" on the front page and then enter your city in the form. A radius search is not supported; the clue must match the specified city. You can also search by state and region (as defined by LbNA), as well as a handful of other options.

Creating clues on LbNA is simple. There is a straightforward one-page form, with far fewer options than on AQ. Note that the LbNA terms of use require that you have permission to place the letterbox.

LbNA allows registered members to log finds and attempts on particular boxes by clicking on the green-flag icon next to the box listing, and to view information on the box that was logged by other members. Unlike AQ, the display of this information

TIP There is a large amount of duplication between clues listed on AQ and LbNA, as many letterboxers choose to list on both. However, some clues are available only on AQ, while others are listed only on LbNA. If you need to know about every box in an area, you will need to check both; otherwise, use the site you are most comfortable with. As for choosing which site to list with, list on both if you care about maximum exposure, or use the one you are comfortable with.

cannot be restricted, and comments are not supported. Like AQ, a "contact the placer" feature is supported.

Valley Quest (http://vitalcommunities.org /ValleyQuest/index.htm)

Valley Quest is believed to be the original North American letterboxing program, predating the "introduction" of the pastime via the *Smithsonian* article by almost a decade. The program operates in the Connecticut River Valley in Vermont and New Hampshire, and its website contains a directory of similar programs around the country.

This description of the program comes from the Valley Quest website: "Questing is a place-based education model of creating and exchanging treasure hunts in order to collect and share your community's distinct natural and cultural heritage—your special places and stories."

Clues are available online and via print publications that can be ordered on the website.

Dartmoor Letterboxing (www.dartmoorletterboxing.org)

This website is a good gateway site to letterboxing where it all began: Dartmoor National Park in England.

Personal and Underground Sites

The letterboxing landscape is replete with personal and underground clue sites, most of which explicitly attempt to avoid exposure. These are usually discovered via word of mouth or accidentally.

Geocaching (www.geocaching.com)
Geocaching is a pastime similar to letterboxing, and there are many crossover participants. Some outdoor enthusiasts who are less interested in rubber stamp art find geocaching more to their liking, and many wish to supplement their letterboxing with an occasional geocache.

LETTERBOXING FORUMS
Most letterboxing discussion occurs on the multitude of forums on Atlas Quest (www.atlasquest.com/boards/boards.html). However, there are several other forums that are worth exploring.

newboxers (http://groups.yahoo.com/group /newboxers)
The newboxers Yahoo group is nominally geared to new letter-boxers, but it has evolved into one of the more important and popular independent letterboxing forums.

LbNA Talk List (http://groups.yahoo.com/group /letterbox-usa)
The LbNA Yahoo group is the oldest North American letterboxing forum on the Internet, dating back to 1998. It has declined in importance over the past few years, though it is

worth joining for hard-core enthusiasts. Its value lies mainly in its archive.

Regional Yahoo groups

There are several regional Yahoo groups for discussing letterboxing in specific areas. While some of that discussion has moved to AQ, leaving certain groups moribund, others are still popular. These groups are listed at www.letterboxing.info /links/?id=75.

Letterboxing on Facebook (www.facebook.com/pages /Letterboxing/112760422071209)

A Facebook page dedicated to letterboxing.

RUBBER STAMP ART SUPPLIES AND TUTORIALS

Carving Media and Tools

Speedball (www.speedballart.com)
Speedball is the creator of the Speedy-Stamp Carving Block ("the pink stuff") carving medium, as well as the linoleum cutters mentioned in this book. They also offer many other tools for rubber stamp artists.

Stampeaz (www.stampeaz.com)
Stampeaz is the creator of PZ Kut and a new medium called Firm Kut.

Most of the carving media, tools, erasers, ink pads, premade stamps, sketchbooks, papers, and various other supplies useful to letterboxers can be bought at major arts and craft stores, such as Dick Blick Art Materials (www.dickblick.com), Michaels Arts & Crafts (www.michaels.com), and MisterArt.com (www.mister art.com).

Atlas Quest also suggests a package deal with most of the carving media mentioned in this book. This can be an excellent option for beginners who are not sure where to start (www .atlasquest.com/marketplace/stampeaz). This is offered through Stampeaz.

Clipart.com (www.clipart.com)

Clipart.com is a huge online repository of royalty-free clip art that can be used as inspiration for rubber stamp images.

Tutorials

There are dozens of tutorials on the web, including some on Atlas Quest. The following are the most comprehensive and detailed that I'm aware of:

Carolyn Hasenfratz's Eraser Carving lesson (www.limegreen news.com/howcarv.html)

Der Mad Stamper's comprehensive guide to inks (www .monkeyhousehobby.com/guides/inkguide)

Custom-Made Rubber Stamps

Several Internet vendors offer custom-made rubber stamps, including RubberStampChamp.com, Stamp-Connection.com, and theStampMaker.com. The latter offers traditional wooden-handled stamps from your artwork. You will never see a stamp like this in a letterbox, and I don't recommend your being the first to create such a stamp for your box, but I offer it as an option for your signature stamp, although this, too, is rarely seen.

Because many stamps used in Dartmoor letterboxing are custom made, Devon Stamps (www.devonstamps.co.uk), a shop based in England, caters to letterboxers.

GEOGRAPHY AND HIKING

Google Earth (http://earth.google.com)

Google Earth is a downloadable application that gives you satellite images of the world, in fairly close-up detail. Some letterboxers find it essential when researching places to plant boxes, or before planning a hunt for boxes. User-supplied pictures of various parks and other points of interest give even more detail of an area and offer a starting point for further research.

Bing Maps (www.bing.com/maps)

Bing Maps is another essential resource for looking in on a box location before visiting it. If the location has "Bird's Eye" viewing available (a little icon will pop up as you zoom in on an area), you will be able to see an area in incredible detail to plan your adventures.

Downloadable USGS Topographical Maps (http://store .usgs.gov)

This U.S. Geological Survey (USGS) site allows you to download free topographical maps (or order print copies) to plan your hikes for letterboxes and geocaches.

Historic Map Works (www.historicmapworks.com)

This site has a huge, browsable collection of old maps. It's useful for creating or researching clues with historical puzzles.

Geographic Names Information System (GNIS; http:// geonames.usgs.gov)

GNIS is a resource for advanced writers of puzzle clues or for geographic problem solvers. It can be used to locate obscure named features mapped by the USGS. Websites such as Google Maps (http://maps.google.com) also have sophisticated geo-locater engines that can find these features. If you need to find an obscure feature that for some reason doesn't show up on a site like Google Maps, try GNIS.

Magnetic Declination Calculator (www.ngdc.noaa.gov /geomag)

This site provides a calculator to determine the magnetic declination at a given location. This is useful if bearings in a clue are given as true and you need to convert them to use a compass, or if you are creating a puzzle with different types of bearings.

Hiking Safety Rules (www.trails.com/list_53_hiking -safety-rules.html)

Letterboxing has brought a lot of non-hikers into the sport of hiking. While many boxes don't require hikes, many do, and it is important to remember that hiking can be a dangerous sport. This website offers a list of safety suggestions to keep in mind before you set out.

CLUE RESEARCH

Internet Anagram Server (www.wordsmith.org/anagram)

This site is a useful resource for constructing or solving anagram puzzles in letterbox clues. Of course, this may be considered "cheating"; it's up to you.

Runic Alphabets (www.omniglot.com/writing/runic.htm)

It would be impossible to list all the websites of this nature that can be used to construct or solve interesting or offbeat clues. This is just one example to get your imagination flowing.

GLOSSARY

Acrostic: A list of words or phrases in which the first letter of each spells another word or phrase.

Anagram: A word or phrase made by transposing the letters of another word or phrase.

Azimuth: See *bearing*.

Back bearing: A technique of reversing or working backward from a given bearing and landmark.

Bearing: Direction on a compass; the number of degrees from magnetic north.

Catching feature: A landmark that indicates to someone following a clue that they have gone too far.

Confirming landmark: A landmark that indicates to someone solving clues or following directions that they are on the right track, or that they have solved a certain portion of the puzzle.

Cootie: A small letterbox (usually just a stamp and sometimes a logbook) hidden on another person or in their gear.

Cuckoo clue: An otherwise unpublished clue found in a letterbox that is moved from box to box.

Direction-of-travel arrow: The arrow on a baseplate compass that indicates the direction to travel after a bearing has been dialed in and the red of the needle is aligned with the red of the orienting arrow.

Exchange: Trading of signature stamp or traveler images between two letterboxers who meet on the trail or at a gathering.

Flea: A cootie that can also be placed in a letterbox like a hitchhiker.

Geocaching: An activity similar to letterboxing in which items are exchanged when a container is found.

GPS: Global Positioning System. An electronic device used to locate any point on the Earth, based on coordinates, to a very high degree of accuracy.

Heading: See *bearing.*

Hitchhiker: A letterbox that is typically only a stamp and log-book and is moved from one host letterbox to another.

Hostel: A letterbox that contains a hitchhiker.

Magnetic declination: The deviation of magnetic north (where compasses point) in a given location, from geographic north (to which most maps are oriented).

Micro box: A very small letterbox, typically in a 35mm film canister.

Mystery box: A letterbox for which the starting location of the hunt is not specified; it must be puzzled out from the clues.

Nib: A carving blade or tip in the Speedball carving system.

Orienting arrow: The arrow in the base of the dial on a base-plate compass that turns along with the dial. It is used to orient the red of the compass needle so that the direction-of-travel arrow is pointing in the direction of the dialed-in bearing.

Pace calibration: A technique that adjusts one person's pace count between two landmarks to another person's pace.

Personal logbook: The logbook or journal a letterboxer carries to collect stamp images from the boxes that are found.

Personal stamp: The stamp a letterboxer carries to stamp into the logbooks of letterboxes that are found.

Poaching: Adding to someone else's letterbox clues that lead to your own box without asking them; that is, the clues to your box use the other person's box as a starting point.

Rebus: A phrase represented by pictures or symbols; the sounds of the images correspond to the sounds of syllables in the phrase.

Signature stamp: The stamp a letterboxer carries to stamp into the logbooks of letterboxes that are found.

Social trail: A new, unofficial trail that develops as a result of continued hiking to the same off-trail location.

SPOR: Suspicious pile of rocks; shorthand for a typical hiding style where rocks need to be piled unnaturally to conceal a box.

Trail name: A letterboxer's nickname or alias used when signing into logbooks or on the Internet.

Traveler: A stamp carried for the purpose of making exchanges with other letterboxers met on the trail.

Triangulation: A technique of using a compass to locate a spot when given two or more sets of landmarks and bearings.

True bearing: Number of degrees from geographic (as opposed to magnetic) north.

INDEX

About the Author

Randy Hall has been letterboxing in North America since 1998 and is a cofounder of the Letterboxing North America website. He was also a nationally ranked orienteer and U.S. Orienteering Team member. He is a finance professional and lives with his family in Chester County, Pennsylvania.